Chocolates

from Steeple Bumpstead

JULIE HAYLOCK

SIDGWICK & JACKSON
LONDON

To all my family,
themselves a selection of sweeties

First published in Great Britain in 1989
by Sidgwick and Jackson Limited
1 Tavistock Chambers, Bloomsbury Way
London WC1A 2SG

Conceived and produced by Swallow Publishing Ltd
260 Pentonville Road, London N1 9JY

Art director: Elaine Partington
Editor: Anne Yelland
Designer: Hilary Krag
Illustrators: Coral Mula, Lucy Su
Photographer: Howard Allman
Stylist: Sarah Wiley
Studio: Del and Co

Typeset by Bournetype, Bournemouth
Origination and printing by Imago Publishing

ISBN 0 283 99877 6

AUTHOR'S ACKNOWLEDGEMENTS

My grateful thanks for the efforts of the Sweet Silk
team – Dean Shanks, Beryl Kemp, Marjorie Thomas,
and Margaret Suckling; also, to everyone at
Swallow Books, especially Anne Yelland, and to
photographer Howard Allman for their patience and
help; and, finally, a special thank you to my sister Penny
whose constant silliness is always a tonic.

Contents

'I have found enormous pleasure in compiling this book and the recipes in it, and I hope that readers will derive as much enjoyment from trying these ideas for themselves.'

Introduction

Chocolate is probably the most popular luxury food. Almost everyone loves to be spoiled with the creamy smooth taste of milk chocolate or the bitter-sweet flavour of plain chocolate. The appeal of chocolate is wide, from the youngest to the oldest members of your family, male or female – age and gender are no barriers.

The challenge of working with chocolate also has its appeal. In this book you will find ideas and recipes for lovely things to make with, serve with, or coat with chocolate. Many are quite delicious without any help but, with the versatility of chocolate, even the simplest sweet or the humblest nut can be transformed into a delight. The reward of producing an array of home-made chocolates for your family and friends is worth all the patience and endeavour necessary to achieve really professional results.

Sweet-making of any kind can produce disasters, but don't be put off. If you follow the rules you will be rewarded and have great fun in the process. There are a few simple points to remember, however:

◆ Do not be in a hurry. Nothing will go right if you try to rush.

◆ Try to choose a dry, cool day. A damp and/or humid atmosphere does not agree with chocolate.

◆ Always have everything to hand before you begin. Once you start, it can spell trouble if you have to stop to look for a measuring spoon or pastry brush.

◆ Buy the best ingredients your budget will run to. You will really be able to taste the difference.

◆ Enjoy what you are doing. Do not be anxious about the results. If your first efforts are not perfect to look at, you will find the encouragement to try again when everyone who tastes them tells you how delicious they are.

All the recipes in this book are tried and tested, and the slightest variation will probably give vastly different results. I suggest that you follow the recipes very carefully to begin with – you will soon discover for yourself those that can be easily varied.

Remember always to treat chocolate gently. If it ever becomes too hot, it will taste strong and burned. If water finds its way into the bowl, it will spoil the results. You will be quite amazed at how the smallest amount of steam escaping from the water below your bowl can change the characteristics of the chocolate in the bowl. Water will change the appearance, the taste and the texture. Finally, with all these recipes, don't be afraid to use your hands. If you cannot dip a truffle or any other sweet because it is too soft (as with a champagne truffle), dip your hands in the melted chocolate and roll the truffle quickly and lightly. This will give a firm coat. Repeat this process more than once if necessary to achieve a good coating of chocolate.

You need not be a dedicated or experienced cook to produce delicious results. Some of the recipes contained in this book are effective but simple. Some will require a little more patience than others, but all will give results that will be pleasing to you and to those who share in the fruits of your labours.

• Equipment •

You will need very little in the way of special equipment to make the sweets and chocolates in this book. If you have a well-equipped kitchen you will probably have almost everything you require.

If there is a single piece of kitchen equipment which you may not have but will certainly find very useful, it is a *cooking* or *sugar thermometer*. You will be much more confident when making sugar-based sweets or sugar syrups if you can accurately follow the stages on a thermometer. It is possible to make sweets without a thermometer, but it really is a worthwhile investment.

The smooth, cold surface of a *marble slab* is a wonderful addition to your kitchen if you wish to make a lot of sweets. However, it is certainly not essential. A laminated board will usually serve the same purpose, although this will not do so well for hot substances. For these, use a large metal tray or baking sheet instead.

A *double boiler*, if you have one, is ideal for melting chocolate in. However, I find that a *heat-proof bowl* which fits snugly over a saucepan works equally well. The bowl needs to be quite large, and it must clear the bottom of the saucepan so that there is a definite space between the water in the pan and the bottom of the bowl (see p. 10).

A strong *heavy-based saucepan* is a must for making sugar-based sweets like fudge. The heavier the saucepan, the more evenly the contents will cook, and even temperatures are most important.

Baking parchment, greaseproof paper, aluminium foil and *heavy-gauge polythene* are all useful for lining tins and placing sweets on to dry and set. Chocolate, once set, will lift easily from a polythene sheet.

Dipping chocolates is much easier if you have a *dipping fork* and *ring*. You can use a dinner fork or cocktail sticks as alternatives, but the end results might not be so attractive.

Moulds, in metal or plastic, for Easter eggs and bunnies and small shapes (hearts, for example) are easy to obtain from specialist cake-making and confectioners' shops. Many large stores now have cookshop departments which also cater for the home confectioner. It is also possible to buy chocolate-making moulds which are deeper, so that a thin chocolate shell may be made, then filled and covered before removing from the mould. Moulds are only necessary if you wish to make a particular type of chocolate novelty – it is possible to make a very good selection of sweets and chocolates without them.

A number of *wooden spoons* with long handles will be an asset. When you are making sweets, you will often be stirring thick bubbling syrups at very high temperatures – the heat will creep up the handle of a metal spoon, making it impossible to hold without a glove.

Paper and foil *petits fours* and *sweet cases* are a lovely finishing touch. Paper cases are available in many colours, although those made with foil hold their shape better, so are more useful for making chocolate cups (see p. 20).

A set of *petits fours* or *aspic cutters* is useful for producing fancy shapes, although small pastry or biscuit cutters will do. These will enable you to make a variety of regular shapes from soft sweets like fondant or marzipan, with very little effort.

An artist's-type *paintbrush* is an invaluable addition to your equipment when making pretty marzipan fruits.

Rice paper is available from stationers and supermarkets, and is useful for some of the recipes in this book.

As you can see, you do not need a lot of expensive equipment – your biggest outlay will probably be your time!

• Introducing chocolate •

Real chocolate is a luxury enjoyed by almost everyone, whatever their age. It is available in many forms, but care must be taken when buying chocolate for home-made confectionery as 'cooking chocolate' is often not chocolate at all, but a substitute that looks quite like chocolate but tastes inferior.

Chocolate is obtained from cocoa beans which are roasted, ground and pressed to produce the pure cocoa mass, cocoa butter and chocolate liquor that form the basis of all chocolate products. At this stage the chocolate is very bitter, but with the addition of sugar and other ingredients (vanilla, milk or milk powder and sometimes a small amount of vegetable fat) it becomes the familiar-tasting confection.

The best type of chocolate to use for the recipes in this book is the rich, dark, dessert-type that is readily available everywhere. You can also use milk or white dessert chocolate for some of the recipes. Many supermarkets sell 'Luxury Chocolate for Cooking' which is available in plain or milk varieties, both of which give excellent results. Always look at the package carefully before you buy. If it is real chocolate, the percentage of cocoa solids contained in the chocolate will be given on the pack. Generally speaking, the higher the percentage of cocoa solids, the richer the chocolate flavour will be. It is also possible to obtain professional confectioners' chocolate or couverture from specialist shops. This has a very high cocoa butter content, and it requires very careful handling to get good results (see p. 12). Specialist confectioners also sometimes sell 'dipping chocolate' which will give a crisp, hard coat.

My advice when buying chocolate for home-made confectionery is always to buy the best that you can afford. Study the package carefully – if the pack says 'chocolate flavoured', it probably does not contain *real* chocolate. Most of the well-known brands of plain, milk and white eating chocolate give very good results in both appearance and taste when used carefully.

You will find that chocolate is available in bars, buttons or drops. Any of these products can be used – the buttons and drops have the advantage that they melt quickly and easily.

◆ The melting process ◆

The most important part of chocolate-making is melting the chocolate correctly. Allow plenty of time. Do not try to hurry the process. If the chocolate is allowed to become too hot, the fats will not combine and the chocolate will lose stability. Its flavour and texture will be spoiled – it will taste strong and burnt – and you will not be able to use it.

Chop the chocolate or break it into small pieces and place it in the top half of a double boiler or in a heat-proof bowl that will fit snugly over a saucepan. Heat about 5cm (2in) of water in the saucepan, making sure that the water does not come into contact with the bottom of the bowl. When the water is almost boiling, turn off the heat, and place the bowl containing the broken chocolate over the hot water. When the chocolate is soft, stir gently with a wooden spoon until smooth. When this stage is reached, remove the bowl from the pan to avoid over-heating the chocolate. If you have a thermometer, check the temperature at this point. It should never go above 50–55°C (122–131°F) and is a good consistency to work with at about 40–45°C (104–113°F).

If you are using the chocolate to dip centres, keep the water in the pan hot, and when the chocolate cools and becomes too thick to use, replace the bowl over the water and warm the chocolate again. Do not be tempted to leave the bowl over the water all the time because the chocolate will continue to heat rather than remain at a constant temperature and this will spoil your results.

◆ Melting chocolate in a microwave oven ◆

It is possible, so long as you take care, to melt small amounts of chocolate using a microwave oven.

Break the chocolate into small pieces, and place them in a non-metallic bowl. Microwave on full power for about 30 seconds at a time. After each 30-second burst, remove the bowl and stir the chocolate. If you allow too long between stirring, you may find that hot spots develop in the bowl, resulting in a little burnt area of chocolate. That will spoil the whole contents of the bowl.

Whichever method you use, be sure always to melt enough chocolate for your requirements. Any that is left can always be melted and used again, and it is very difficult to dip centres in too shallow a pool of chocolate. This can sometimes be overcome by transferring the last of the chocolate from the bowl into a warmed tall glass (see p. 42).

• Tempering •

If you can obtain, and choose to use, couverture, it is essential that you have a thermometer to check the temperature at the various stages of tempering. Tempering is necessary because of the high proportion of cocoa butter and other fats in couverture. This process stabilizes the fats in the chocolate to give a crisp, glossy finish when dry.

You will need a saucepan and bowl as for melting chocolate. The temperatures given here are suitable for the most popular dark or plain couverture. If you are using milk, then the temperatures at all stages should be reduced by about 2°C (4°F).

1 Break the couverture into even-sized pieces. Begin the melting process, and place a thermometer into the couverture. Stir the chocolate as it melts, keeping a close eye on the temperature.

2 Allow the chocolate to reach a temperature between 45°C (113°F) and 50°C (122°F). Remove the bowl from the pan. With the thermometer still in position, cool the chocolate quickly by plunging the base of the bowl into very cold water. *Do not allow water to come into contact with couverture.*

3 When the temperature of the couverture reaches 25–27°C (77–81°F), return the bowl to the pan of hot water. Raise the temperature once more – this time to 31–32°C (88–90°F).

4 Remove from heat. The couverture is now ready to use.

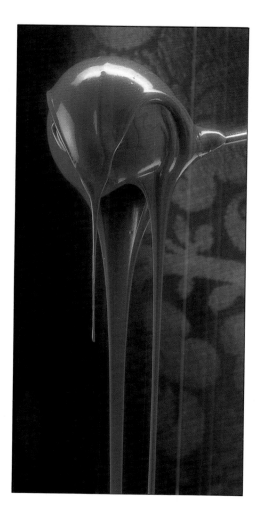

———————— ◆ ————————

I find this is the simplest way of tempering a small amount of couverture. If you are going to be using large amounts, it is probably worth investing in a marble slab. With one of these, you can cool the couverture quickly and evenly by pouring about two-thirds of the melted chocolate on to the slab, then working it towards the middle with a spatula, until the temperature reaches

• How to temper couverture •

The term tempering applies to the method of controlled raising and lowering of temperatures necessary when using specialist 'couverture'. It is quite a difficult procedure to master, but it is absolutely necessary if you are going to use couverture for your chocolates. It might take one or two attempts to get it right, so, to begin with, do not try using too much. It is imperative that you use a thermometer to monitor each stage closely.

At the initial melting stage, the couverture should reach about 47 °C (116 °F), so a clearly marked thermometer is essential. Stir gently while melting.

With small amounts of couverture, reduce the temperature by plunging the bowl into cold water. Be sure no water comes over the top of the bowl.

If you wish to temper a larger amount of couverture, you can reduce the temperature more quickly by pouring about two-thirds of the melted chocolate from the bowl on to a marble slab.

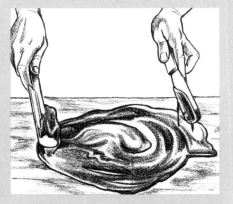

Work the couverture from the outside towards the centre until it just begins to set. You will have to work quickly to return the cool couverture to the remaining, still warm, chocolate.

about 24°C (75°F). Quickly return the cooled couverture to the bowl and mix thoroughly with the remaining third, checking the temperature as you do so. When the overall temperature is about 32°C (90°F), it is ready to use.

The tempering process is quite time-consuming and takes practice to get it absolutely right. You need only temper *couverture*: dessert or eating chocolate or cooking chocolate can be used after gently melting to a liquid form.

POINTS TO REMEMBER

◆ Do not attempt to melt chocolate over direct heat.

◆ Chocolate burns easily, so take care even when you are using a bowl over hot water.

◆ Never allow water or steam to come into contact with chocolate. This will result in the chocolate becoming stiff and grainy.

◆ Essential oils and essences ◆

These are very important in the making of good sweets. Do not use artificial flavours, as these will often give unsatisfactory results. The richness of a natural flavour is unmistakable. They are usually quite expensive, but you need only add very little as they are powerful. Most high-class supermarkets will have peppermint, almond, vanilla and orange essences. You may have to search in specialist confectioners' shops for some of the less common essences, like violet, strawberry and lemon.

◆ Colourings ◆

It is now possible to buy food colourings in the form of powders or pastes, as well as the more common liquids. Powder is far better for colouring white chocolate as it reduces the need to add liquid, which can make the chocolate thick and difficult to handle.

◆ Basic ingredients ◆

Although chocolate is the most important ingredient in home chocolate-making, basic ingredients – milk, butter, sugar, and so on – cannot be ignored.

Butter Always use unsalted butter for your confectionery. You can taste the salt even in the slightly salted varieties.

Sugar Generally, you can use granulated or caster sugar when sugar is specified. You will also need icing sugar for some of the recipes.

Milk Use whole milk rather than the skimmed or semi-skimmed varieties. Whole milk gives more body to the finished sweets.

Glucose Liquid glucose (glucose syrup) can be a bit difficult to work with, but it will make finished mixtures easier to handle. Rather like golden syrup, it is easier to measure liquid glucose if you *just* warm the syrup first. Also use warm spoons and a warm knife to measure and scrape with.

Chocolate Moulds and Cases

Moulding chocolate shapes is a relatively simple process, so a good introduction to chocolate-making if you have never tried it before. You will usually get very good results if you use commercially available moulds (to make an Easter egg, for example, or a selection of chocolate animals), and follow the advice given here on how to use them. You do not have to use moulds, however, to make a selection of delicious and professional-looking chocolates. It is possible to use sweet cases as moulds, paint chocolate inside them, and fill them with a variety of centres. In this section, details of how to use moulds, how to make and fill chocolate cups, and how to hand-mould chocolate shapes are given, and advice offered on how to get good results every time.

• Moulding •

Many different types of moulds are now available for use in making confectionery. You can buy metal or plastic moulds, both large and small. Some are intended for making solid chocolate shapes – little animals, flowers, leaves, bows – others are for making larger shapes – hollow eggs, rabbits, heart-shapes, and so on.

Whatever type of mould you use, there is one basic rule which applies to them all: *moulds must be scrupulously clean.* Several days before you intend to use your mould, wash it thoroughly in washing-up liquid. Rinse well, and dry on a clean, soft cloth. Leave the mould in a warm place to dry completely. Although it may feel dry, there is a danger that some moisture may have been left in the cracks and corners. Immediately before you use it, polish the inside of the mould with clean cottonwool. Do not touch the inside of the mould with your fingers or you may get a mark on your finished item and even the smallest amount of oil from the skin may cause problems when you come to unmould your chocolate. You do not have to wash the mould each time you use it, so, if you only have a mould for one half of an Easter egg and you wish to make two or more, as long as you do not touch the inside of the mould between fillings, you can reuse it without any problems.

When you have completed your moulding and have an array of shapes and figures, take care to protect them from damp and humidity. Also, if you wish to

Moulded Easter eggs, decorated with sugar flowers and presented in baskets, and Easter bunnies, together with moulded baskets filled with a selection of truffles and hand-moulded roses (foreground) and tiny eggs. Small moulded eggs also fill the bought basket in the background.

· Making an Easter egg ·

Home-made Easter eggs are fun to make and give. With a little practice, using moulds becomes quite simple. The mould must be clean and completely dry and the chocolate not hot but warm and fluid. Be sure to melt plenty of chocolate for the mould you are using. Have too much rather than not enough as it is easier to fill the mould right to the rim, allow a few minutes setting time, then pour out the excess.

Fill the mould to the rim before pouring off the excess chocolate. It is important to have plenty of chocolate in any case so that you can swirl a good coating all around the inside of the mould.

Pour out excess chocolate and scrape across the flat face of the mould with a palette knife. Turn the mould over and leave to dry. Repeat the whole procedure to give a double thickness of chocolate.

Carefully remove from the mould. If you wish to join two half eggs together, paint a little melted chocolate around the rim of one half.

Gently position the second half while the rim of chocolate is still wet. Handle the finished egg as little as possible – wear gloves if necessary.

handle the moulded items, to decorate an Easter egg, for instance, it is a good idea to wear light cotton gloves to avoid marking the surface.

When moulding, it is important to have enough chocolate for the job. It is always best to melt far more than you think you will need. Any chocolate that is left will not be wasted; simply allow it to harden, wrap it and reuse it next time.

Generally speaking, plain chocolate is easier to mould than any other. A child, however, will usually prefer the sweeter taste of milk chocolate, so a compromise of half milk, half plain chocolate might be best.

◆ Moulded baskets ◆

Baskets and bowls, which can be filled with chocolates or other sweets, or perhaps marzipan fruits for a gift, are useful shapes to be able to mould. They can also be served with fresh fruit and cream or ice-cream to offer as a special dessert.

It is possible to buy moulds for baskets and use them in the same way as Easter egg moulds. Adding a handle will complete the basket. To do this, measure across the width of the finished basket, then with moulding chocolate (see p. 24) form a handle whose base fits the width of the basket. The handle will be stronger if you divide the moulding chocolate into three thin strips, then very carefully plait it until you have the right length. Bend it carefully into shape and leave it so that the chocolate hardens before you attach it to the basket with a little melted chocolate.

If you do not have a suitable mould, you can use any suitably shaped bowl or dish as a mould. Metal bowls are easier to use than glass, and plastic will also give good results. Make sure the bowl is clean and dry, and polish it with cottonwool as you would any mould. Fill it with melted chocolate, leave it for about five minutes, then pour out the excess. Allow it to harden completely, when it should have shrunk away from the sides slightly, making it easy to remove from the bowl.

Remember that you will get a slightly larger finished chocolate shape if you mould the chocolate outside the bowl. Dip it in melted chocolate, then turn it upside-down. Dip at least twice, and touch up around the edge with a brush to ensure that you get a good shape. Allow the chocolate to harden before you attempt to remove the chocolate shape. This may take a little longer than a regular moulded shape.

◆ Easter egg ◆

These directions will give good results with any type of large hollow mould including chocolate boxes and Valentine's hearts, for example. This amount of chocolate will be enough to make both halves of a medium-sized Easter egg.

675g (1½lb) plain chocolate
or 340g (12oz) milk, 340g (12oz) plain chocolate

◆

1 Melt the chocolate in a bowl over a pan of hot water, as described on p. 10.

2 Polish the inside of the mould with clean cottonwool. Hold the mould near the bowl and, using a large spoon, fill it with chocolate.

3 Take a palette knife and tap the sides of the egg several times. Pour out the excess chocolate and invert the mould on to a sheet of baking parchment or polythene and allow it to set. If you are using a metal mould, the chocolate will set quite quickly. In a plastic mould, it might take a little longer.

4 As the chocolate sets it will shrink away from the sides of the mould very slightly, so it should pop out of the mould quite easily. If it does not, put the mould in the refrigerator for a while, then try again. You might find it necessary to twist the mould slightly, but you should never use force as the chocolate shape will easily break.

5 Repeat the procedure for the other half of the egg.

If you have two halves of a shape to fit together, follow the directions on p. 16. Remember, though, that half an Easter egg can be filled with home-made chocolates and used as a gift-box.

With a little practice, it is possible to mould figures in dark chocolate with white areas inset, for example, a Father Christmas in dark chocolate with a white beard. Use a small spoon to fill that part of the mould with melted white chocolate, then allow it to set hard before continuing as before.

• Moulding small, solid chocolates •

These basic guidelines will enable you to use most types of mould successfully. You can also use almost any household dish or container as a mould so long as it is clean and dry – the top of a jam-jar for flat circles, for example. Allow chocolate to set completely before removing the mould.

1 Be sure to have enough chocolate melted. Polish the inside of the mould with cottonwool.

2 If the shapes are set into one larger frame, hold the mould close to the chocolate and, using a large spoon, fill the little shapes with the melted chocolate. Tilt the mould slightly towards the bowl so that any excess rolls into the bowl.

3 Take a palette knife and scrape across the surface of the mould to remove any chocolate that remains on the face of the mould. Now take the mould firmly in both hands and tap it lightly, several times, on a work surface to remove any air bubbles. Put the mould in a cool place to set.

4 If the moulds are individual shapes (that is, not in one frame), carefully fill each mould, smooth the top of the mould, tap the sides once or twice with the palette knife, then stand in a cool place to dry.

• Chocolate cups •

If you want to make chocolates with liquid, or very soft centres, and you do not have a suitable mould, you can make little cups using petits fours or sweet cases. Choose foil

Moulded chocolate boxes like this Valentine's heart, filled with more chocolates, make lovely gifts. One or two chocolates wrapped in gold foil add a further touch of luxury.

◆ Hand-made chocolate cups ◆

Very soft or liquid centres can be enclosed in little individual cups made using simple paper or foil sweet cases. Foil cases, although not as easy to come by as paper ones, do hold their shape better.

If you have a small brush, use that to coat the inside of the cup. The rounded handle of a teaspoon will also give reasonable results. Allow the first chocolate coat to dry and harden before applying at least one more coat.

Be sure to make the lids large enough, otherwise the filling might seep out. The lids should also be of an even thickness – not thick in the centre with thinner edges as the edges might crack when the lids are attached to the cups.

Remove the foil case from the cup when the chocolate is completely set. Fill at least three-quarters full, then tap the bottom of the cup gently on a flat surface to disperse any air bubbles. Allow to settle for a few minutes.

Paint a rim of melted chocolate around the lid. Position quickly, pressing gently to ensure that it sticks. Leave to set completely before turning the chocolates over so that the lid becomes the base. Decorate, if you wish (see pp. 86 and 88).

cases if possible; if you have to use paper ones, keep several inside one another to strengthen the top one. Milk, plain and white chocolate are all suitable.

MAKES ABOUT 25 CUPS
450g (1lb) chocolate
petits fours cases
non-stick baking parchment

◆

1 Measure the petits fours cases across their widest part and, on the baking parchment, draw 25 circles that size, to make little lids for the chocolates.

2 Melt the chocolate in a bowl over a pan of hot water, as described on p. 10.

3 Keep the petits fours cases in stacks of about five or six together. Drop a spoonful of melted chocolate into the top case: the other cases will help to keep the shape.

4 Spread the chocolate to cover the inside of the case completely. Repeat until you have coated 25 cases.

5 Starting with the first case you completed, repeat the process a second time on each case. When all the cases are done, put them to one side to set, while you make the lids.

6 Put a teaspoonful of chocolate on one of the little circles you have drawn on the parchment. Using the back of the spoon, spread the chocolate evenly over the circle. Continue until you have 25 lids.

7 When the chocolate cases are cold and firm, carefully remove the paper cases from the outside. The cases are now ready to fill.

8 When the cups are filled, lift the lids very carefully from the parchment. Have a little melted chocolate to hand. One at a time, attach the lids. Allow the cases to become firm – this does not take long.

◆ Liqueur cups ◆

Although tempting, it is not a good idea to fill chocolate cups with neat liqueurs; adding them to a sugar syrup, or mixing them with a little fondant or marzipan, gives much better results. The sugar syrup here can be used with liqueurs or spirits, and is suitable for liquid fillings for all small moulded chocolates. A thin sugar coat will form on the inside of the chocolate, leaving the centre deliciously fluid.

TO FILL 25 CUPS
375g (12oz) granulated sugar
90ml (4fl oz) cold water
60ml (4tbsp) liqueur of your choice

◆

1 Combine the sugar and water in a heavy-based saucepan and stir continuously over a low heat until the sugar has dissolved. If any crystals of sugar remain on the side of the pan, dip a pastry brush in cold water, and brush them down into the syrup. Test for undissolved sugar as described on p. 44.

2 Increase the heat to moderate and allow the syrup to boil until it reaches a temperature of 108°C (225°F). Immediately remove the pan from the heat and place it in cold water to arrest the cooking process.

3 Have a second saucepan, or large jug, to hand. Add the liqueur to the

syrup, but do not stir it in. Instead, pour the syrup backwards and forwards from saucepan to saucepan (or jug). This reduces the risk of sugar crystals forming in the syrup. When the liqueur is incorporated into the syrup, cover with cling film and leave until cold.

4 Once it is cold, the syrup can be used to fill the cups.

------◆------

VARIATIONS

Fondant cups Strong spirits like brandy and rum complement the smooth sweetness of fondant. For 25 cups, you will need ½ recipe fondant (see pp. 64–6), and 45ml (3tbsp) brandy or rum. Knead the spirit into the fondant, then use it to fill the cups. This produces a runny, syrup-type filling.

Marzipan cups To fill 25 cups, you will need ½ recipe orange marzipan (see p. 29), and 45ml (3tbsp) orange liqueur (cointreau or grand marnier). Knead the liqueur into the marzipan, then use it to fill the cups.

Cherry cups Maraschino cherries make their own liqueur if wrapped in fondant first. Put a spoonful of soft fondant into the chocolate cup, place a maraschino cherry inside, then another spoonful of fondant before sealing.

Ginger cups Preserved ginger makes an interesting filling. Use the syrup in the jar and chop the pieces of ginger well. Pack the chopped ginger into the case, then spoon a little of the syrup over before sealing.

◆ Creamy chocolate cups ◆

This recipe for a rich and creamy chocolate filling is simple and adaptable. This filling is best for cups or shells made using a mould, since these are normally smaller than those made with sweet cases, although foil sweet cases, which are normally smaller than paper ones could also be used. It is rather rich for a large cup of the sort produced with most paper sweet cases. Also, it is better to have ready-made lids for the cases, rather than run melted chocolate over the top of the cases, because the filling is fluid and will remain so. You could, if you prefer, fill the moulded cups and chill them for at least an hour, when it should be possible to seal them with melted chocolate.

TO FILL ABOUT 25 CUPS OR SHELLS
170g (6oz) plain chocolate
70ml (3fl oz) double cream
15ml (1tbsp) glucose syrup

------◆------

1 Chop the chocolate into small pieces and place in a heat-proof bowl.
2 Place the double cream and glucose syrup in a small saucepan and bring to the boil. Pour over the chopped chocolate and leave to stand, without stirring, for about one minute.
3 Stir until all the chocolate is melted,

and allow to cool. Make sure it is cool before you use it.
4 The filling can be varied as described below but is very acceptable left as it is. It is better to fill an icing bag and pipe the mixture into the cups or shells, as it is difficult to spoon it in neatly. Chocolates made with fillings of

A selection of small, solid moulded chocolate shapes (foreground), and hand-made and filled chocolate cases, which can also be decorated with a contrasting chocolate.

this type are best eaten within three or four days.

VARIATIONS

Once the mixture is cool, it can be varied by the addition of any of the following: 15ml (1tbsp) cointreau and the grated rind of one small orange; 25g (1oz) chopped hazelnuts (or add a whole hazelnut to each cup); 30ml (2tbsp) armagnac or kirsch.

Fruit flavourings also work well with this type of filling but I find it better to use milk rather than plain chocolate, since this makes a lighter base. Try to choose the sharper, more defined fruit flavours as these are less likely to become lost in the richness of the base. Raspberry, strawberry, and cherry are all suitable; really tangy fruit flavours such as lemon or pineapple would oppose the chocolate taste, and so are best avoided.

◆ Chocolate shells ◆

The fillings above all work equally well with chocolate shells, for which it is possible to buy moulds. The finished chocolates made with these moulds will be slightly larger.

1 Coat the mould two or three times, as described on p. 18, pouring away the excess each time. Allow the chocolate to set completely.

2 Spoon in the filling, not quite to the top of the chocolate. Seal the tops with more chocolate and allow to set before removing the shells from the mould.

◆ Chocolate for hand moulding ◆

If you want to make a chocolate shape for which a mould is not available, flowers or some animals, for instance, it is possible to hand-mould chocolate. Animals – cats, dogs, chicks, teddy bears, and so on – can be hand-moulded very successfully. I always find it best to exaggerate features like eyes and ears to give the animals an appealing look. Where possible, give the creature a 'surprised' expression, with raised eyebrows and a little open mouth. You can also give them almost any style of hat – bowlers, bonnets, boaters or berets – again made from moulding chocolate; once these are firm, add ribbons and flowers to complete the effect. Chocolate flowers, too, with or without the addition of chocolate leaves (see p. 92), make attractive decorations for chocolates, petits fours and desserts.

MAKES 175–225G (6–8oz)
140g (5oz) plain chocolate
90ml (4fl oz) liquid glucose

————————◆————————

1 Melt the chocolate in a bowl over a pan of hot water, as described on p. 10. Add the liquid glucose, and stir the mixture well to combine. Form into a ball and wrap in cling film. Allow the chocolate to rest in the refrigerator for several hours.

2 When you are ready to use the chocolate, take it from the refrigerator and uncover. If it is too hard to mould, let it come to room temperature, but do not allow it to become too warm or it will be too sticky to handle. It should be solid but pliable, slightly oily and 'tacky'.

◆ Moulding a chocolate rose ◆

Hand-moulded flowers and figures are rewarding to make. Little chocolate roses (and rose leaves, see p. 92) make charming cake decorations and give a really professional appearance to desserts and to Easter eggs. It is best not to be too adventurous at first – make one or two quite large roses to begin with, until you are familiar with the way moulding chocolate behaves.

Take a piece of moulding chocolate and form it into a cone about 12mm (½in) high and thicker at the bottom than the top. Roll several more pieces into small balls – these will form the petals.

Make the petals by pressing the balls of chocolate between your forefinger and thumb until they are thin and rounded. Make the first two the same size, the next two slightly larger, and so on.

Wrap the bottom of each petal around the cone base and gently press the pieces together. Continue in this way, positioning each petal so that it overlaps the previous one slightly.

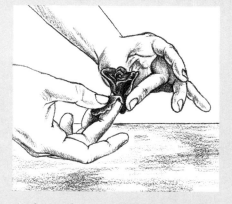

As the rose forms, carefully curl back the edges of the petals to make the finished flower as open or as bud-like as you wish. Place the finished rose gently aside and leave to set.

Petits Fours

Petits fours are small and dainty sweet things served after a meal. They can be made of chocolate, marzipan, cake, biscuit, or fruit – in fact almost anything small and sweet. It is best to serve a variety of petits fours, as everyone likes to have a choice of something plain, like a mint, or something more exciting – a brandy snap with rich fillings, perhaps. In the selection of recipes that follows all the petits fours are based on, or include, either marzipan or chocolate. Marzipan is a wonderfully versatile confection. It can be moulded and coloured easily, it can be flavoured, or have fruit and nuts added to give a variety of petits fours. The chocolate petits fours range from simple flavoured chocolate thins to delicious crumbly florentines. Many people expect petits fours to be luxurious and liqueur-laced, but there are those who prefer neither. A lot of the suggestions that follow, therefore, are suitable for varying in many ways so that you can offer something to suit most tastes. All the recipes included in this section, however, are suitable for serving as petits fours in the true sense.

• Marzipan •

Marzipan is easy to make at home, but many shop-bought marzipans are excellent and you can often choose between 'golden' or 'white' finishes. The white is far better for colouring to make marzipan fruits and petits fours. The more easily available yellow or golden is traditionally used for cakes, and is perfectly acceptable for flavouring or for mixing with other interesting textures. It also makes a delicious centre for dipping simply as it is.

In order to colour marzipan successfully, it is necessary to use it at room temperature or slightly warmer. It is almost impossible to work with very cold marzipan. It is, however, important to avoid over-handling, as the marzipan will become oily and sticky. Remember, too, that pale pastel colours look best in marzipan. Always err on the side of caution when colouring any food as a paler appearance than you intended is far better than a dark red or green, which will not appeal to the eye.

It is a good idea to allow marzipan to 'rest' in a cool place between stages, and always keep it covered or wrapped when it is not being used, as it quickly forms a 'crust' as it dries.

It will take a little patience and practice, but once you have mastered the technique of handling and colouring marzipan, with a little imagination you can produce a wide variety of shapes and colours, some of which might in addition be dipped, or partially dipped, in chocolate.

Marzipan fruits to try – orange and water melon slices, bananas, apples, pears, oranges, lemons, cherries and strawberries. Caster sugar, cloves and angelica add the finishing touches.

26

✦ Colourless marzipan ✦

The addition of a little liquid glucose to the basic ingredients gives a lighter, more malleable, marzipan. This is the best recipe to use for marzipan fruits (see p. 30) or for any shape for which hand modelling is necessary.

MAKES ABOUT 1KG (2¼LB)
450g (1lb) icing sugar, sifted
450g (1lb) ground almonds
5ml (1tsp) liquid glucose
2 egg whites, lightly beaten

1 Place the icing sugar and ground almonds in a large bowl and stir to combine. Add the liquid glucose and enough lightly beaten egg white to bind.
2 Knead gently by hand. If the marzipan becomes 'tacky', sift a little more icing sugar over the work surface as you knead.
3 Gently form the marzipan into a ball, wrap it in cling film, and allow it to rest in a cool place for one to two hours before use.

✦ Traditional marzipan ✦

The egg yolk in this recipe will give a degree of colour but if you prefer marzipan with a more golden colour, add a drop or two of yellow food colouring with the egg yolk.

MAKES ABOUT 400G (14OZ)
225g (8oz) ground almonds
115g (4oz) caster sugar
115g (4oz) icing sugar, sifted
1 large egg yolk, beaten
juice of half a lemon
a few drops of almond essence

1 Place the ground almonds, caster sugar and icing sugar in a large bowl and stir to combine thoroughly.

2 Mix together the egg yolk, lemon juice and almond essence, and add enough of the egg mixture to the dry ingredients to bind them together.
3 Knead lightly by hand until the paste is pliable. Avoid over-handling at this stage or the marzipan may become oily and difficult to work with.
4 Gently form into a ball, wrap in cling film, and allow to rest for about one hour before use.

• Orange marzipan •

This is a pleasant-tasting, less almondy marzipan than the other recipes, which I find is especially nice when used to stuff dates. No eggs are used in this recipe, so it is very suitable for the young or the elderly or those with egg-related allergies. The orange flavour is very light and subtle, but you could increase this, if you wish, with the addition of a little orange oil or essence or indeed orange liqueur.

MAKES ABOUT 400G (14oz)
115g (4oz) icing sugar
115g (4oz) caster sugar
115g (4oz) ground almonds
1 large orange
a few drops of orange colouring (optional)

◆

1 Finely grate the rind from the orange. (It is a good idea to leave the orange in the refrigerator for an hour or two beforehand, as this makes grating the rind much easier.)
2 Squeeze the juice from the orange, and measure about 30ml (2tbsp).
3 Mix the icing sugar, caster sugar and ground almonds together in a large bowl. Add the rind, and enough orange juice to bind the ingredients together.
4 Knead lightly. Add a little orange colouring if required.
5 Gently form into a ball, wrap in cling film, and allow to rest for about one hour before use.

• Marzipan petits fours •

These are simple and quick to make, yet give impressive results. A combination of a few of these ideas, packed in a presentation box, makes a pleasing gift. Alternatively, arranged on a dainty plate, they make a stylish and tempting way to finish a meal.

• Cherry rolls •

Some liqueurs impart a wonderful flavour to marzipan, but it is important not to make the finished result too wet. I find soaking fruits in the liqueur for a few hours, then kneading them into the marzipan is the best way to overcome this.

MAKES 20–24 PETITS FOURS
50g (2oz) glacé cherries, chopped
30ml (2tbsp) kirsch or sherry
225g (8oz) colourless marzipan (see p. 28)
a little pink colouring
cornflour, to dust

◆

1 Soak the cherries in the liqueur. Colour half the marzipan pale pink, then knead the cherry and liqueur mixture into the marzipan.

· Marzipan fruits ·

Miniature fruits made with marzipan are always a well-received gift. It is, of course, possible to flavour the marzipan with the taste of the fruit it resembles, although this may not seem worth while with very tiny fruits. Large fruits, however, make an interesting centrepiece for a buffet table when arranged in a fruit bowl or basket, and are more successful flavoured.

Knead the marzipan lightly until pliable. Add the colouring very carefully. By using a cocktail stick it is possible to push colouring into the body of marzipan – this will help you to achieve an even colour not a marbled effect.

Knead again after adding colouring. Add more if necessary but take care not to make the colour too strong. Knead gently, using your fingertips if possible to avoid over-handling the marzipan which could cause oiliness.

Handle only lightly when shaping the fruits. If your hands become warm while you are working, dust them with a little cornflour.

Add finishing touches like cloves or angelica immediately the fruits are made, but let them dry before painting, if necessary.

2 On a cornflour-dusted surface, roll the remaining marzipan into an oblong about 15 × 17.5cm (6 × 7in). Press the cherry marzipan on to this oblong and flatten them together with your hands.

Roll up, Swiss-roll style, wrap in cling film, and allow to rest in a cool place for about an hour.

3 Remove the cling film, and cut into 12mm (½in) slices.

• Marzipan dates •

These marzipan dates make a sumptuous change from the traditional Christmas dates. Serve them with walnut halves sandwiched together with marzipan for a real treat.

MAKES 20–24 PETITS FOURS
225g (8oz) dates
175g (6oz) marzipan
30ml (2tbsp) dark rum
115g (4oz) plain chocolate

◆

1 Remove the stones from the dates.
2 Knead the rum evenly through the marzipan, then use the marzipan to stuff the dates, pushing them gently back into shape round the filling.

3 Melt the chocolate in a bowl over a pan of hot water, as described on p. 10. Allow to cool, then dip each end of the dates in the chocolate, leaving the middle section uncovered.

• Nutty marzipan •

The flaked almonds contained in this recipe give a crunchy texture without varying the basic almond taste. However, chopped walnuts or hazelnuts can be used in their place to give texture and a subtle flavour to this marzipan.

MAKES 20–24 PETITS FOURS
225g (8oz) colourless marzipan (see p. 28)
a little yellow food colouring
50g (2oz) flaked almonds
cornflour, to dust

◆

1 Colour the marzipan a delicate yellow. Toast the almonds lightly until golden, then chop them roughly.
2 Knead the almonds into the marzipan.

3 On a surface lightly dusted with cornflour, roll out the marzipan to about 12mm (½in) thick. Cut into rounds or other shapes using biscuit or petits fours cutters.

• Marzipan fruits •

With a little ingenuity and application, it is possible to make almost any type of 'fruit' from marzipan, but remember to use food colourings *sparingly*. It is better to have slightly pale-looking fruit, as too much colour looks unappetizing. A good selection to start with might include apples, oranges, bananas, pears, strawberries, and lemons.

MAKES A SELECTION OF FRUITS
450g (1lb) colourless marzipan (see p. 28)
60g (2oz) icing sugar
60g (2oz) cornflour
red, yellow, green, pink,
orange and dark brown food colouring
a few whole cloves
angelica
— ◆ —

1 Divide the marzipan into six roughly equal pieces (about 60–90g/2–3oz). Take two pieces to colour green, for apples and pears. Wrap the remaining pieces until you need them.

2 Sieve the icing sugar and cornflour together. Use it to dust a flat working surface as necessary.

3 Knead, colour and shape the marzipan, as shown on p. 30.

4 Use cloves for the bases of apples and pears, and angelica for stalks. Stand the fruits on greaseproof paper and allow to dry for an hour.

5 When the fruits are dry to the touch, take an artist's small brush, and carefully blush the apples with a light pink colouring to give a ripening effect. The same should be done with the pears, but use a pale orange colouring to blush these. Allow to dry thoroughly before packing in an airtight container.

Follow the same basic method for the rest of the fruits.

———————— ◆ ————————

OTHER FRUITS TO TRY

Oranges and lemons Finish oranges by pushing a clove into the base. Roll the finished fruits gently over a fine cheese-grater to give the appearance of orange peel. Finish lemons in a similar way but omit the clove.

Bananas Finish bananas by painting on dark brown 'tips' and lines. They always tend to look more realistic if you give them an over-ripe appearance.

Strawberries Finish strawberries by pricking all over with a cocktail stick, then sprinkle with caster sugar. Make a tiny angelica stalk for each strawberry, and cut green marzipan leaves.

◆ Chocolate petits fours ◆

Generally, these will take a little longer to prepare than those made with marzipan, especially if you take into account that the basic marzipan can be made in advance. The addition of some chocolate petits fours in the selection you offer, though, will increase the appeal of all of them.

◆ Florentines ◆

Although these delicious, crumbly yet crunchy little biscuits can be made larger and used as a teatime treat, they are traditionally served as, and make an interesting addition to a selection of, petits fours.

· Neatening and finishing florentines ·

The smallest amount of flour is enough to bind together all the good things that make these florentines so special. It is important to remember to space them well apart on the baking sheets – cook them in batches of four or six at a time, both to give them plenty of room to spread and to allow yourself enough time to neaten them while they are still hot. Trying to finish more than six at a time takes a lot of practice!

Use a teaspoon to measure small amounts of the well-combined mixture on to a greased or lined baking sheet. If necessary flatten the mixture with a damp palette knife.

Take care not to overcook. Once you have removed them from the oven, work quickly with a knife or palette knife to neaten the still hot florentines, pushing them into small rounds.

When the florentines are cold, melt the chocolate. Allow it to cool and thicken slightly before you spread it over the flat side of the florentines.

The traditional marking is easy to achieve by drawing a dinner fork across the chocolate in a 'wavy' movement. Do this before the chocolate sets.

MAKES ABOUT 25 PETITS FOURS
60g (2oz) unsalted butter
60g (2oz) light soft brown sugar
60g (2oz) flaked almonds, chopped
60g (2oz) glacé cherries, chopped
30g (1oz) mixed peel, chopped
30g (1oz) plain flour, sifted
140g (5oz) plain chocolate, melted

1 Preheat the oven to 180°C/350°F/ gas mark 4, and grease two large baking sheets very well, or cover them with non-stick baking parchment.

2 In a medium-sized saucepan, melt the butter over a low heat. Add the brown sugar and stir until the sugar has dissolved. Test for undissolved sugar as described on p. 44.

3 Remove from the heat and add the almonds, cherries, and peel. Mix thoroughly, then stir in the flour and beat the mixture well to combine.

4 Drop small amounts of the mixture on to the baking sheets, then bake for about 8–10 minutes until golden brown. Remove from the oven and quickly neaten with the palette knife.

5 Allow to cool for a minute or two, then transfer the florentines on to a wire rack to cool completely.

6 When the florentines are cold, carefully turn them over and coat with chocolate as shown on p. 33.

◆ Chocolate florentines ◆

These are easy to make and can be served with or instead of the biscuit-type florentines. As there is no baking involved, these are quick to produce, and are an ideal way to use up a little left-over chocolate. If you are unsure of your ability to make neat circles with a teaspoon, you could use the clean tops of jam-jars to make even-sized discs. Add the fruit and nuts while the chocolate is still warm, but allow it to set hard before removing the lids. Almost any type of fruit and nuts can be used in the topping – try walnut pieces, unsalted peanuts, large flakes of coconut, chopped dates, chopped crystallized fruit, peel or sultanas for this recipe. The important point to remember is vary the size and colours of the fruit and nut topping.

MAKES ABOUT 25 PETITS FOURS
140g (5oz) plain chocolate
60g (2oz) whole nuts (brazils, almonds, hazelnuts)
60g (2oz) coloured glacé cherries, quartered
60g (2oz) seedless raisins

1 Line a baking tray with non-stick parchment or polythene.

2 Melt the chocolate in a bowl over a pan of hot water, as described on p. 10.

Allow it to cool slightly and thicken.

3 Drop a teaspoonful of chocolate on to the tray and, with the back of the spoon, swirl it into a flat disc about 4cm

Mint and orange after-dinner thins, made with plain and milk chocolate, with a plate of crumbly traditional and plain chocolate florentines in the foreground.

(1½in) across. Immediately push a whole nut, two pieces of glacé cherry and two raisins into the chocolate disc.

4 Continue in this fashion until all the chocolate is used. Do not try to make more than one at a time as the chocolate will harden too much to allow the fruit and nuts to stick to it.

◆ After-dinner thins ◆

Serve these wafer-thin chocolate crisps with coffee after a meal, or pack them into a pretty box for an unusual and acceptable gift.

A chocolate mould for round, flat discs is perfect for these, but if you don't have one, you can get very satisfactory results by drawing on your patience to form little circles with a spoon. It is very important to use natural oils and not flavourings when making these chocolate thins, as a drop or two of natural oil will be easily absorbed into the chocolate and give a wonderful flavour. If you try to add an artificial flavouring compound, you will need to add far more to the chocolate to get the same results. The chocolate will reject the addition of this liquid and become thick and stiff and difficult to handle. Also, there is no comparison between the two in taste.

MAKES ABOUT 25 THINS
140g (5oz) plain chocolate
30g (1oz) granulated sugar
a few drops of peppermint oil

1 Line a large tray with a sheet of thick polythene.

2 Melt the chocolate in a bowl over a pan of hot water, as described on p. 10. Remove the bowl from the pan and stir in the sugar.

3 Add a drop or two of peppermint oil and stir gently but thoroughly into the chocolate.

4 With a teaspoon, drop small amounts of the mint mixture on to the polythene. With the back of the spoon, swirl the chocolate round to make a wafer-thin disc. Allow the chocolate to dry completely before lifting the mints from the polythene very gently, using the blade of a palette knife.

VARIATIONS

Milk chocolate mint thins If you prefer, you can use milk chocolate to produce these mint thins. Milk chocolate thins will take longer to dry than those made with plain chocolate, but alternate milk and plain chocolate thins arranged on a dish to serve do look very appealing.

Orange thins You can make orange after-dinner thins by using a few drops of natural orange oil instead of peppermint oil. For the reasons given above, a flavouring compound will not give good results. I usually make orange thins from milk chocolate and mint thins from plain. If you do make both, be sure to serve and store them separately as the mint will take over the flavour of the orange and spoil the taste.

Thin coffee crisps Search for a good coffee essence and use a few drops of that in place of peppermint or orange oil. Some coffee essences can be a little bitter, so it might be necessary to add a little more sugar. I think plain chocolate works better than milk with the flavour of coffee, so a little additional sugar will remove a touch of bitterness without making the end result too sweet.

• Brandy snaps with creamy chocolate filling •

Brandy snaps make lovely petits fours and can be filled with lightly whipped fresh cream, perhaps laced with a tablespoon of rum or brandy. The creamy chocolate filling suggested here is lovely and light, yet luxurious and different.

MAKES 25–30 PETITS FOURS
90g (3oz) unsalted butter, diced
60g (2oz) caster sugar
45ml (3tbsp) golden syrup
60g (2oz) plain flour, sifted
5g (1tsp) ground ginger

CREAMY CHOCOLATE FILLING
170g (6oz) plain chocolate, melted
60g (2oz) unsalted butter, diced and softened
1 egg, separated
70ml (3fl oz) double cream

1 Preheat the oven 180°C/350°C/ gas mark 4.

2 Place the butter, sugar and golden syrup in a medium-sized saucepan and stir over a low heat until the butter melts. Remove from the heat.

3 Add the flour, about a third at a time. Finally, stir in the ginger and mix well.

4 Grease two or three baking sheets well. Drop small spoonsful of the mixture on to the baking sheets, leaving 50–75mm (2–3in) space around each one. The brandy snaps will spread out as they cook.

5 Cook one sheet at a time in the centre of the oven for about 8–10 minutes, or until the brandy snaps are an even golden brown in colour. Meanwhile grease the handles of two wooden spoons.

6 Remove the first tray from the oven and place the second one in. Allow the cooked brandy snaps to cool for about 30 seconds, then loosen each one with a flat knife. Working quickly, roll the brandy snaps one at a time around the spoon handles. They will cool quickly. Allow them to become just firm before you remove the spoon. Place on a wire rack until cold.

Repeat with all the biscuits.

7 At this stage, it is possible to keep the brandy snaps in an airtight tin for about a week.

8 For the filling, cool the melted chocolate slightly, then add the softened butter. Beat the egg yolk lightly and stir into the chocolate mixture.

9 Whisk the egg white until thick. Carefully fold it into the chocolate. Whip the double cream lightly – until it just holds its shape. Fold gently into the mixture.

10 Fill the brandy snaps with the cream immediately before you intend to serve them.

VARIATION

Mocca cream Melt 60g (2oz) plain chocolate, as described on p. 10. Dissolve 10g (2tsp) instant coffee powder in 15ml (1tbsp) hot water. When cool, add to the chocolate. Allow to cool but not set. Lightly whip 140ml (6fl oz) double cream, then gently fold in 25g (1oz) sifted icing sugar. Fold the melted chocolate into the cream. Chill for about an hour. Fill the brandy snaps when ready to serve.

Chocolate-based Sweets

Recipes which include chocolate in the ingredients will often be delicious without the necessity of a further chocolate coating. All the recipes in this section are made using chocolate, although none of the finished sweets is actually dipped in chocolate. Sometimes the addition of only a few grams or ounces of chocolate is enough to produce a rich, luxury confection. The taste of the chocolate seems to be emphasized by the cooking process, but there are also recipes which require no cooking and are quick and easy to produce, the addition of a little melted chocolate enhancing both flavour and appearance.

• Rocky road •

'Rocky road' is an American-style sweet, originally made by melting chocolate and mixing in nuts and marshmallows. In the recipe that follows, the nuts and marshmallows are mixed into a rich, chocolatey fudge to give delicious and eye-catching results. You could achieve a fuller flavour, without losing the distinctive appearance, by substituting plain for milk chocolate, and using half golden syrup and half black treacle instead of the golden syrup. Try using nuts with a more prominent taste, too, like chopped walnuts in place of the peanuts. The result will be a rich, dark fudge with a stronger flavour. It is most important to remember that the fudge must be cool before the marshmallows are added. If not, they will melt away completely as you stir them in. If the fudge has become too stiff when it is cool to enable you to stir the marshmallows in, then spread half of the mixture into the prepared tin, scatter the chopped marshmallows over, then spread the remaining fudge gently over the top.

MAKES ABOUT 800G (1¾LB)
450g (1lb) granulated sugar
300ml (10fl oz) whole milk
90g (3oz) unsalted butter
30ml (2tbsp) golden syrup
5ml (1tsp) vanilla essence
90g (3oz) milk chocolate
60g (2oz) marshmallows, roughly chopped
115g (4oz) whole peanuts, skins removed

♦

1 Oil a 20cm (8in) square baking tin, and line the bottom with baking parchment.

2 In a large, heavy-based saucepan, combine all the ingredients except the chocolate, marshmallows and peanuts.

A selection of sweets made with chocolate: American-style rocky road fudge, made with marshmallows and peanuts, on the right rich and creamy milk chocolate fudge, and Beryl's chocolate crunch (foreground), a quick and easy no-cook recipe.

3 Place the pan over a low heat, and stir the mixture gently with a wooden spoon until all the sugar has dissolved and the butter melted. Test for undissolved sugar, as described on p. 44.

4 Raise the heat slightly and bring the mixture to a steady boil. Stirring from time to time, allow the fudge to boil until the temperature reaches 114–115°C (237–239°F), or the 'soft ball' stage (see p. 45).

5 Meanwhile, melt the chocolate in a bowl over a pan of hot water, as described on p. 10.

6 Remove the fudge from the heat. Allow to stand and cool for about one minute, then stir in the melted chocolate. Beat the fudge until it starts to thicken, then stir in the nuts. Continue to stir until quite cool, then fold in the marshmallows. Turn the fudge into the prepared tin.

7 As you have made so many additions to the fudge, do not attempt to mark it prior to cutting. When it is completely cold, just turn it out and, using a large, long-bladed knife, cut the fudge into squares. You will not get neat and regular pieces of fudge, but the appearance is characteristic of the confection, and synonymous with the name 'rocky road'.

◆ <u>Rich chocolate fudge</u> ◆

This creamy-rich confection is enjoyed by both adults and children. This fudge's wonderful chocolate flavour is not really improved by an additional chocolate coating.

MAKES ABOUT 675G (1½LB)
450g (1lb) granulated sugar
250ml (8fl oz) whole milk
150ml (5fl oz) unsweetened evaporated milk
90ml (4fl oz) double cream
90g (3oz) unsalted butter
115g (4oz) milk chocolate

◆

1 Lightly oil a 20cm (8in) square baking tin, and line the bottom with baking parchment.

2 In a large, heavy-based saucepan, combine the sugar, milk, evaporated milk, and double cream. Dice the butter and add to the pan. If you have a sugar thermometer, place it in the pan at this stage.

3 Place the pan over a low heat, and stir the mixture constantly with a wooden spoon until all the sugar has dissolved and the butter melted. Test for undissolved sugar as described on p. 44.

4 Raise the heat slightly and bring the mixture to a steady boil, stirring frequently. Take extra care here as it is quite easy to burn fudge with such a high milk and cream content.

5 Meanwhile, melt the chocolate in a bowl over a pan of hot water, as described on p. 10.

6 When the temperature of the fudge reaches 114–115°C (237–239°F), or the 'soft ball' stage (see p. 45), remove the pan from the heat and beat the mixture for one minute.

7 Beat in the melted chocolate and continue to beat until the chocolate is evenly distributed and the fudge appears thick and creamy. Turn the fudge into the prepared tin. When almost set, mark into squares.

8 When the fudge is cold and firm, turn it out of the tin and remove the parchment. Cut into squares as marked.

• Nutty fudge •

This recipe is quick, easy to make, and cut into slices makes a popular and unusual party treat for children. For the adult members of the family it is probably better cut into little squares and presented in sweet cases.

MAKES ABOUT 800G (1¾LB)
115g (4oz) plain chocolate
60g (2oz) unsalted butter, softened
70ml (3fl oz) unsweetened evaporated milk
115g (4oz) hazelnuts, chopped
450g (1lb) icing sugar, sifted

1 Lightly oil a shallow baking tin about 25×20cm (10×8in).
2 Melt the chocolate in a bowl over a pan of hot water, as described on p. 10. Remove the bowl from the saucepan and stir the chocolate until it begins to cool. Stir in the butter a little at a time, then add the evaporated milk in the same manner. Mix thoroughly to combine. Add the hazelnuts, then gradually add the icing sugar.
3 When all the ingredients are well combined, press the mixture into the prepared tin.
4 Allow to set completely before cutting into fingers or squares.

• Beryl's chocolate crunch •

Beryl Kemp has been with me since I started my chocolate-making madness! She has become a good friend, as has this recipe of hers. Like the previous recipe, this does not require cooking and, for adults, is best cut into small squares.

MAKES ABOUT 560G (1¼LB)
225g (8oz) digestive biscuits
115g (4oz) butter or margarine
30ml (2tbsp) golden syrup
180g (6oz) plain chocolate
30g (1oz) chopped nuts

1 Lightly grease a baking tin about 20cm (8in) square.
2 Crush the biscuits finely – either use a food processor or place them in an unsealed polythene bag, a few at a time, and use a rolling pin to crush them.
3 Place butter or margarine in a saucepan with the golden syrup and heat until just melted.
4 Melt 90g (3oz) of the chocolate in a bowl over a pan or hot water, as described on p. 10. Add to the saucepan, then stir in the crushed biscuits. Mix well to combine thoroughly.
5 Press the mixture into the prepared tin, spreading it evenly with a flat-bladed knife. Chill until set.
6 When the base is quite firm, melt the remaining 90g (3oz) chocolate as before, and pour over the biscuit mixture.
7 While the chocolate topping is still warm, sprinkle the nuts over. Mark into squares or slices at once. Cut when cold.

Dipping Chocolates

With the addition of a chocolate coating, almost any sweet food can become a treat and a luxury. The simplest of centres – whole brazil nuts or a punnet of fresh strawberries, for example, see pp. 54 and 56 – take on a new and unexpected identity with the help of a little chocolate and, of course, more intricate centres are welcomed by both adults and children. In this section, you will find advice on how to dip almost any kind of centre, hard or soft, in chocolate, along with recipes for suitable centres for dipping. Most of these recipes are also delicious in their own right, and do not necessarily need the addition of a chocolate coating to make them so. Many of the recipes in other sections of this book are also suitable for dipping in chocolate, if you follow the basic guidelines given here.

◆ How to dip sweets ◆

In order to dip centres in chocolate successfully, it is important to be sure that you have enough melted chocolate to cover any centre completely and easily when it is dropped into the bowl. When you have dipped a number of centres, and the reservoir of chocolate is getting low, transfer the remaining chocolate to a warmed jug or tumbler, so that the pool of chocolate is deeper. This will make it easier to dip.

You will find it much easier to dip chocolates if you have a set of dipping forks. These are available from cookshops and hardware stores. They are normally sold in pairs, that is, one fork with two or three prongs, and a dipping ring. As you become proficient at dipping centres, you will be able to mark and decorate the finished chocolates with the dipping tools as you go along. If you do not have a dipping fork, you could use a carving or fondue fork, or even a large table fork, with reasonable results.

To begin with, do not attempt to dip difficult shapes. Use even, thick and firm centres. Of course, you will be able to dip fancy shapes and softer centres after a time, but it is annoying and frustrating if a soft centre melts or a fancy shape ends up looking like a featureless blob. Until you have had a little practice, my advice is to stick to simple shapes and firm sweets.

Allow plenty of time. As with all things culinary, if you are in a hurry, nothing goes right. Melt the chocolate carefully (see p. 10) and try to keep it at a constant temperature. Have ready several sheets of parchment or heavy polythene. As you dip the centres, place them on the sheets in a line, working from the top and coming towards you. Try not to pass over finished centres in order to place freshly dipped centres on the paper.

It is best to have a variety of centres ready for dipping. They should be at room temperature and quite dry. If the centres are damp, the chocolate will not cover evenly. If they are sticky, you will have problems when you come to remove the finished chocolate from the fork.

• Dipping soft centres •

Coating a soft centre in chocolate takes a little patience and practice and is better attempted after you have become confident at dipping firmer sweets or nuts. Softer centres do add variety to your chocolate selection, however. To dip soft centres successfully, the chocolate should be slightly cool but not thick. If you are dipping jellies or jelly-based sweets like Turkish delight, warm chocolate may cause them to begin to dissolve so take extra care.

Hold the sweet gently but firmly between your fingers, and dip the bottom of it into the chocolate. Allow the liquid chocolate to drain off.

Draw the partially dipped sweet across the rim of the bowl gently so that you do not scrape the chocolate away. Allow the sweet to dry chocolate side up.

When the chocolate is quite firm, drop the sweet into the melted chocolate. Push it gently down until it is coated. Lift from the bowl by putting your fork under the double-coated foot.

With the aid of a flat-bladed knife, carefully ease the dipped sweet from the fork on to a sheet of parchment or polythene. Allow the chocolate to set completely before moving.

• Dipping hard centres •

It is best to start with a basic square, firm sweet to dip, and a bowl of carefully melted chocolate. Toffees and caramels are good to begin with, and brazil nuts or stuffed dates also make successful choices.

1 Drop the sweet into the chocolate and turn it over using the fork. When you are sure that the centre is completely covered, lift it out of the chocolate with the fork.

2 Tap the fork smartly on the side of the bowl so that the excess chocolate falls away, then draw the bottom of the fork across the lip of the bowl to remove any accumulation underneath the sweet.

3 Place the dipped chocolate on to a sheet of parchment or polythene to dry. If the chocolate seems reluctant to slip from the fork, gently ease it off using a flat-bladed knife.

4 For round sweets, use a dipping ring as the metal ring is usually thicker than the prongs of a dipping fork, and will not so readily penetrate the sweet itself as you dip.

5 Work your way through your selection of centres, returning the bowl of chocolate to the pan to reheat when necessary. (It is a good idea to have some nuts and raisins or some chopped nuts among your selection so that you can use up the last of the chocolate, see p. 54.)

6 Leave the dipped chocolates in a cool, dry place for several hours to set completely. The setting process can be hurried along by placing them in the refrigerator, but you will get a better finish on the chocolate if you allow it to set and dry naturally.

• Vanilla fudge •

This is a good basic fudge recipe that can be added to or varied quite successfully. Although some of the fudge recipes that follow at first sight may look similar to this basic one, there are differences between them. Follow the directions in the individual recipes closely for perfect results.

Makes about 675g (1½lb)
450g (1lb) granulated sugar
250ml (8fl oz) whole milk
300ml (10fl oz) unsweetened evaporated milk
90g (3oz) unsalted butter, diced
vanilla essence

———•———

1 Oil a 20cm (8in) square baking tin, and line the bottom with baking parchment.

2 In a large, heavy-based saucepan, combine the sugar, milk, evaporated milk, and butter. If you have a sugar thermometer, place it in the pan at this stage.

3 Place the pan over a low heat and stir the mixture gently with a wooden spoon until all the sugar has dissolved and the butter melted. Test for undissolved sugar by tapping the bottom of the pan with the spoon. If there is a slight 'crunching', the sugar has not quite dissolved and you should continue to stir for a little longer.

4 Raise the heat slightly. Boil steadily, stirring frequently, until the fudge reaches a temperature of

44

• Making fudge •

Soft and sweet, fudge symbolizes all that home-made confectionery should be. It is not difficult to make and can be varied simply or dramatically. A sugar thermometer makes controlling the temperature and cooking time much easier, but it is possible to test the stage the fudge has reached without one if necessary. It is most important to dissolve the sugar completely. If any accumulates on the sides of the pan, brush it back into the mixture with a pastry brush dipped in warm water. Raise the temperature to speed the cooking process only after the sugar has dissolved.

To test without a thermometer, remove the pan from the heat. Drop a small spoonful of fudge into a bowl of cold water. Leave for a few seconds.

If the fudge is at the 'soft-ball' stage (about 114–115°C/237–239°F), you should be able to press the mixture together with your fingers.

Beat the mixture in the pan until it thickens, then pour it into the prepared tin. Spread evenly.

Marking the fudge into squares when it is almost set makes it easier to cut once it is cold and firm.

114–115°C (237–239°F), or the 'soft ball' stage (see p. 45).

5 Remove the pan from the heat and stir in the vanilla essence (or other flavouring). Beat the fudge until it begins to thicken and look cloudy. Turn the fudge into the prepared tin. When almost set, mark into squares.

6 When the fudge is cold and firm, turn it out of the tin and remove the parchment. Cut into squares as marked.

◆

VARIATIONS

Omit the vanilla essence and use about 10ml (2tsp) coffee essence instead. Alternatively, add 90g (3oz) finely chopped walnuts or blanched almonds. Always make any additions to fudge after it has reached its highest temperature.

◆ Creamy vanilla fudge ◆

This is a rich and luxurious recipe. The fudge is delicious with or without a chocolate coating, but if you are using it as a chocolate centre, cut it into very *small* pieces as it is such a rich sweet. The creamy taste of this fudge should be complemented by the vanilla essence, not overpowered by it, so don't be tempted to add too much – I find that eight drops are just about right.

MAKES ABOUT 675G (1½LB)
450g (1lb) caster sugar
150ml (5fl oz) whole milk
300ml (10fl oz) double cream
90g (3oz) unsalted butter
60ml (4tbsp) cold water
8 drops of vanilla essence

◆

1 Oil a 20cm (8in) square baking tin, and line the bottom with baking parchment.

2 In a large, heavy-based saucepan, combine the sugar, milk, and cream. Dice the butter and add to the pan with the water and vanilla. If you have a sugar thermometer, place it in the pan at this stage.

3 Place the pan over a low heat and stir the mixture constantly with a wooden spoon until all the sugar has dissolved and the butter melted. Test for undissolved sugar, as described on p. 44.

4 Raise the heat slightly, but be very careful not to burn the fudge. Stir gently and frequently until the fudge reaches a temperature of 115°C (239°F), or the 'soft ball' stage (see p. 45). This slightly higher temperature gives a better setting quality to such a soft fudge.

5 Remove the pan from the heat. Leave to stand for a minute, then beat the mixture gently with the wooden spoon until the fudge begins to thicken. Turn it into the prepared tin. When the fudge is almost set, mark into small squares.

6 When the fudge is cold and firm (you may find it necessary to chill it to achieve this – place it in the refrigerator once it is cool), turn it out of the tin and remove the parchment. Cut into squares as marked.

Rum and raisin fudge, with orange and cinnamon fudge and, a variation on the basic vanilla fudge recipe, cherry fudge. In the foreground is a plate of sweet and crumbly melting montelimar.

46

• Rum and raisin fudge •

Rich and fruity, this is a favourite recipe with the grown-up members of the family. The raisins can be made plump and succulent by soaking overnight in fruit juice or a little extra rum. This fudge is also the basis for a lovely Christmas treat.

MAKES ABOUT 675G (1½LB)
450g (1lb) granulated sugar
400g (14oz) sweetened full-cream condensed milk
60g (2oz) unsalted butter, diced
45ml (3tbsp) dark rum, made up to 150ml (5fl oz) with cold water
115g (4oz) seedless raisins

1 Oil a 20cm (8in) square baking tin, and line the bottom with baking parchment.
2 In a large, heavy-based saucepan, combine the sugar, condensed milk, butter, and rum and water. If you have a sugar thermometer, place it in the pan at this stage.
3 Place the pan over a low heat and stir the mixture constantly with a wooden spoon until all the sugar has dissolved and the butter melted. Test for undissolved sugar as described on p. 44.

4 Raise the heat and bring the mixture to a steady boil, stirring frequently until the fudge reaches a temperature of 114–115°C (237–239°F), or the 'soft ball' stage (see p. 45).
5 Remove the pan from the heat. Leave to stand for a minute, then stir in the raisins. Turn the fudge into the prepared tin. When it is almost set, mark into squares.
6 When the fudge is cold and firm, turn it out of the tin and remove the parchment. Cut into squares as marked.

• Walnut and maple syrup fudge •

This is an interesting combination with the subtle sweetness of the maple syrup blending with the obvious crunchiness of the walnuts. It is a lovely fudge to eat as it is, but if you want to coat it in chocolate, you should halve the amount of maple syrup.

MAKES ABOUT 675G (1½LB)
450g (1lb) granulated sugar
250ml (8fl oz) whole milk
300ml (10fl oz) unsweetened evaporated milk
90g (3oz) unsalted butter
30ml (2tbsp) maple syrup
60g (2oz) walnuts, coarsely chopped

1 Oil a 20cm (8in) square baking tin, and line the bottom with baking parchment.
2 In a large, heavy-based saucepan, combine the sugar, milk and evaporated milk. Dice the butter and add to the

saucepan. If you have a sugar thermometer, place it in the pan at this stage.
3 Place the pan over a low heat and stir the mixture with a wooden spoon until all the sugar has dissolved and the

butter melted. Test for undissolved sugar as described on p. 44.

4 Raise the heat slightly and bring the mixture to a rapid boil. Boil steadily, stirring occasionally at first, then more frequently to prevent it burning, until the fudge reaches a temperature of 114–115°C (237–239°F), or the 'soft ball' stage (see p. 45).

5 Remove the pan from the heat, and beat in the maple syrup. Continue to beat until the mixture begins to thicken and appear 'grainy'. Stir in the walnuts.

Turn the fudge into the prepared tin. When almost set, mark into squares.

6 When the fudge is cold and firm, turn it out of the tin and remove the parchment. Cut into squares as marked.

◆

Note: Adding the maple syrup at the last minute means that under certain conditions you will find it necessary to chill this fudge to achieve a really firm set. Place it in the refrigerator once it is cool.

◆ Orange and cinnamon fudge ◆

A lovely spicy fudge with an unexpected tang, this makes an unusual dipping centre, but is very good without a chocolate coating. The recipe produces a firm but more crumbly type of fudge. It is best to use a thermometer for this fudge as it needs to be boiled to a very slightly higher temperature than 'soft ball' might indicate. The addition of fruit juice might otherwise prevent the fudge from setting. If the fudge is boiled to 115°C (239°F) instead of between 114°C (237°F) and 115°C (239°F), the addition of the juice will only retard the setting process.

MAKES ABOUT 675G (1½LB)
450g (1lb) granulated sugar
250ml (8fl oz) whole milk
250ml (8fl oz) unsweetened evaporated milk
5ml (1tsp) cinnamon
90g (3oz) unsalted butter, diced
*finely grated rind and 45ml (3tbsp) strained
juice from one large orange*

◆

1 Oil a 20cm (8in) square baking tin and line the bottom with baking parchment.

2 In a large, heavy-based saucepan, combine the sugar, milk, evaporated milk, and cinnamon. Add the butter.

3 Place the pan over a low heat and stir the mixture gently with a wooden spoon until all the sugar has dissolved and the butter melted. Test for undissolved sugar, as described on p. 44.

4 Raise the heat and, stirring from time to time, bring the mixture to a rolling boil. Stir more frequently now

with the wooden spoon to prevent the fudge from sticking. Continue to boil the mixture until the temperature reaches 115°C (239°F).

5 Remove from the heat immediately. Allow the fudge to cool for two to three minutes, then stir in the orange rind and juice. Mix thoroughly. Beat the fudge for a minute or two, then turn into the prepared tin. When it is almost set, mark into squares.

6 When the fudge has set completely and is quite firm, turn it out of the tin, and remove the parchment. Cut into squares as marked.

• Melting montelimar •

Montelimar is usually a fruit- and nut-packed nougat-like confection. This recipe will produce a confection that has a sweet and crumbly texture that is almost meringue-like, and has an attractive appearance.

MAKES ABOUT 675G (1½LB)
450g (1lb) granulated sugar
150ml (5fl oz) water
150ml (6tbsp) clear honey
3 medium egg whites
a pinch of cream of tartar
2.5ml (½tsp) vanilla essence
90g (3oz) icing sugar, sifted
60g (2oz) blanched, flaked almonds, roughly chopped
60g (2oz) hazelnuts, roughly chopped
60g (2oz) glacé cherries (assorted colours), roughly chopped
rice paper
——◆——

1 Combine the granulated sugar and water in a heavy-based saucepan and stir over a low heat until the sugar has dissolved. Test for undissolved sugar, as described on p. 44.

2 Bring to the boil, stirring occasionally, until the temperature reaches 138°C (280°F). Meanwhile, heat the honey in a second saucepan, and bring to a brisk boil.

3 Whisk the egg whites in a heat-proof bowl until they are stiff.

4 When the sugar syrup reaches 138°C (280°F), remove from the heat, add the cream of tartar and stir well. Beating constantly, gradually add the syrup to the egg whites. Beat in the honey, then add the vanilla essence.

5 Carefully stir in the icing sugar, then add the nuts and cherries. Allow to cool very slightly.

6 Line a 20cm (8in) square baking tin with rice paper. Spoon the mixture over the rice paper and smooth the top. Cover with rice paper. Leave to cool for about 20 minutes, then cover with a board and weight well – you could use the weights from the kitchen scales or a pile of books does as well. Leave the montelimar weighted for at least 12 hours. Remove the weights, turn out of the tin and cut into bars or squares.

• Uncooked coconut ice •

Coconut ice is another favourite sweet which can be prepared quickly and easily. It is possible to vary the flavour or colour whether you use this recipe or the cooked variety. Traditionally, coconut ice is pink and white, but it is not absolutely necessary to add any colour as the finished confection is very pleasant left white. This recipe produces a soft and smooth texture that is almost fondant-like.

You could, as an alternative, make mint ice by flavouring half the coconut mix with peppermint oil and colouring it green. Leave the first half white.

Coconut ice is traditionally coloured, often pink and white or green and white, as here. Green and white ice can also be flavoured with a few drops of peppermint oil.

MAKES ABOUT 900G (2LB)
575g (1¼lb) icing sugar
400g (14oz) sweetened full-cream condensed milk
450g (1lb) unsweetened desiccated coconut
a few drops of pink food colouring

1 Put half of the icing sugar in a bowl. Add half of the condensed milk and mix thoroughly. Now add half of the coconut. The mixture will be thick and stiff and very difficult to stir. Turn out on to an icing-sugar-dusted board and shape the mixture into a rectangle about 20×15cm (8×6in). Cover with a clean, dampened tea-towel.

2 Put the second half of the icing sugar in the bowl. Add the remaining condensed milk and a few drops of pink food colouring. Mix thoroughly. Add the rest of the coconut and again mix thoroughly.

3 Remove the tea-towel from the first rectangle, and press the pink mixture on top of the white.

4 Allow to set, then, using a sharp knife, cut into slices or squares.

VARIATION
Orange and lemon ice Follow the basic recipe, but omit the pink colouring and add a few drops of orange flavouring and colour to one half and a few drops of lemon flavouring and yellow colouring to the other half. Leave to set, then cut as before.

◆ Cooked coconut ice ◆

This produces a firmer coconut ice with a slightly crunchy texture. Although still creamy, the finished coconut ice is not as soft and delicate as the uncooked variety. It is also easy to make and takes less effort to mix.

MAKES ABOUT 675G (1½LB)
450g (1lb) granulated sugar
150ml (5fl oz) whole milk
170g (6oz) unsweetened desiccated coconut
15ml (1tbsp) double cream
a few drops of pink food colouring

1 Oil a 20cm (8in) square baking tin and line the bottom with baking parchment.

2 In a large, heavy-based saucepan, combine the sugar and milk. If you have a sugar thermometer, place it in the pan at this stage.

3 Heat slowly, stirring constantly, until all the sugar has dissolved. Test for undissolved sugar, as described on p. 44.

4 Raise the heat. Boil briskly, stirring frequently, until the mixture reaches a temperature of 114–115°C (237–239°F), or the 'soft ball' stage (see p. 45).

5 Remove the pan from the heat and stir in the coconut and cream. Beat vigorously. Pour or spoon half the mixture into the prepared tin. Add a few drops of pink colouring to the remaining half of the mixture, and stir until evenly coloured. Press this mixture on to the top of the first layer in the tin.

6 Allow to cool completely and set, then cut into squares or bars.

◆ Creamy caramel ◆

This caramel makes an excellent dipping centre, and the chocolate coating also removes the problem of keeping the air from the finished sweet. If you do not coat this caramel in chocolate, you must wrap each piece separately in waxed paper.

MAKES ABOUT 450G (1LB)
60g (2oz) unsalted butter
280g (10oz) granulated sugar
30ml (2tbsp) golden syrup
300ml (10fl oz) double cream
5ml (1tsp) vanilla essence

1 Line a 20cm (8in) square baking tin with greaseproof paper, and use half the butter to grease the paper.

2 In a large, heavy-based saucepan combine the sugar, golden syrup, cream, and remaining butter. Place the sugar thermometer in the pan at this stage.

3 Place the pan over a medium-low heat, and stir the mixture with a wooden spoon until all the sugar has dissolved and the butter melted. Test for undissolved sugar, as described on p. 44.

4 Bring the mixture to the boil, stirring only occasionally, until the temperature reaches 121°C (250°F).

5 Remove the pan from the heat and stir in the vanilla essence. Turn the caramel into the prepared tin and set aside to cool.

6 When the caramel is cold and firm, turn it out of the tin and remove the greaseproof paper. Oil the blade of a strong knife and use this to cut the caramel into pieces.

◆ Crunchy chocolate toffee ◆

You could also spread melted chocolate over this toffee while it is still in the tin. If you do not coat it in chocolate, you must wrap each piece.

MAKES ABOUT 675G (1½LB)
225g (8oz) light soft brown sugar
30ml (2tbsp) water
170g (6oz) unsalted butter
60g (2oz) almonds, chopped

1 Grease a shallow baking tin about 23cm (9in) square.

2 In a large, heavy-based saucepan combine the sugar, water, and butter. Place the sugar thermometer in the pan at this stage.

3 Place the pan over a medium-low heat, and stir the mixture with a wooden spoon until all the sugar has dissolved and the butter melted. Test for undissolved sugar, as described on p. 44.

4 Boil the mixture steadily, stirring only occasionally, until the temperature reaches 140°C (284°F).

5 Remove the pan from the heat and stir in the chopped nuts. Turn the toffee into the prepared tin and leave to set.

6 When cold and hard, turn out of the tin and break into pieces with a rolling pin.

Fresh Fruit and Nuts

Fruit and nuts make attractive and unusual petits fours. You will find advice here on dipping various kinds of fresh fruit and nuts in chocolate for a refreshing and pleasant end to a summer dinner party. Bear in mind when dipping fresh fruit, however, that it will not keep even overnight – you must serve these fruits on the day you prepare them. In addition, there are more time-consuming recipes for crystallized fruit and peel, and frosted and glacé fruits. Crystallized fruit and peel can also be dipped in chocolate, if you wish, but are attractive and pleasant-tasting left as they are. The most important point to remember when using fruit for any of the recipes in this section is that it should be in perfect condition, ripe but firm, and as fresh as possible.

• Dipped nuts •

Whole brazil nuts, half walnuts, whole hazelnuts or almonds, all look good simply dipped in melted chocolate and brazil nuts, in particular, are delicious Christmas favourites. It is best to buy ready shelled nuts.

MAKES ABOUT 450G (1LB)
225g (8oz) shelled nuts
about 225-280g (8-10oz) chocolate

———————◆———————

1 Melt the chocolate in a bowl over a pan of hot water, as described on p. 10.
2 Dip the nuts using a dipping ring as described in Dipping hard centres on p. 44. If they are a bit small, it is always possible to dip them twice, allowing them to dry thoroughly after each dipping. This will increase the size of the finished chocolate (and help you get a selection of even-sized chocolates), without affecting the taste of the nut.

———————◆———————

VARIATION
Another nice nutty centre can be made by removing the stones from dates, and replacing them with a brazil nut. Push the date back into shape, then dip.

• Nut clusters •

These are lovely little sweets to add to a selection of petits fours, and are simple and quick to make. They are also an ideal way to use up chopped or broken nuts, and any left-over melted chocolate.

A plate of part-dipped fresh fruits – including strawberries, kumquats, plums, physalis and star fruit – and half walnuts and whole brazil nuts completely dipped in chocolate, garnished with chocolate rose leaves.

1 Stir the nuts into the chocolate, and add some raisins or sultanas. Stir round in the chocolate so that they are completely coated.

2 Remove from the chocolate with a teaspoon, and shape into little clusters. Leave to set on a sheet of parchment or heavy polythene.

◆ Coating fruit in chocolate ◆

It is best not to cover fruits completely in chocolate, but to part-dip them. Choose fruits with care. Use only fresh and firm fruits, and wash them only if necessary. Dry thoroughly. Where possible, leave stems attached, and do not hull strawberries or peel grapes. Small whole fruits like strawberries, grapes and cherries are probably the best to use, but if you follow the advice here, you can dip most fruits successfully. If you are coating a selection, leave those such as apple slices until last, so that if their 'dampness' affects the behaviour of the chocolate, you will not have to struggle with the appearance of the easier fruits.

170g (6oz) plain chocolate
225–340g (8–12oz) prepared fruits
◆

1 Melt the chocolate in a bowl over a pan of hot water, as described on p. 10.
2 Be sure that the chocolate is fluid, but cool, before dipping.

———————◆———————

DIPPING FRESH FRUITS
Strawberries, grapes and cherries If possible, hold the fruit by the stem. If the stems have been removed, push a cocktail stick into the very top of the fruit and use it to hold the fruit while you dip. Gently dip the fruit into the chocolate to cover half to three-quarters of the fruit. Stand on polythene or parchment to dry. (Alternatively, to avoid getting a flat 'bottom' to the chocolate, hold the fruit until it is dry.)

Orange and tangerine segments These are fine to use, but take care that the thin membrane around each segment is unbroken, because if any fruit juice finds its way into the chocolate, it will become difficult to work with and may spoil your end results. Hold the segments gently in your fingers as you dip them. Coat half to three-quarters of the fruit in chocolate, and allow to dry.

Kiwi or star fruit Juicy soft fruits such as these should be sliced and have chocolate drizzled over them. Peel and slice the fruit. Dry on absorbent paper, then place on parchment or greaseproof paper. Spoon some chocolate into a piping bag with a fine writing nozzle attached, or a paper piping bag, and using a side to side motion, drizzle the chocolate in lines over the fruit. Alternatively, sprinkle star fruit with lemon juice and dip the points in chocolate.

Apple and pear slices These should be the last fruits dipped. Sprinkle them liberally with lemon juice to preserve the colour. Dip the slices as orange and tangerine segments.

• Crystallized fruits •

Crystallized or candied fruits will keep for a long time, and you can achieve very good results at home, although the process is quite lengthy. Strengthening and reboiling the sugar syrup does not in itself take long, but the whole process must be done slowly and will take about seven to ten days to complete. When crystallizing fruit it is important to use only one type of fruit at a time. If you try to mix two or more types in the same syrup, the flavours will be impaired. The recipe that follows is for canned fruit, which, because it has been in a syrup before you start, will crystallize faster than fresh fruit. Pineapple pieces look especially attractive when crystallized, and make a good starting point for anyone who is a little nervous about embarking on the process.

450g (1lb) canned fruit (drained weight)
450–900g (1–2lb) granulated sugar

———————————————◆———————————————

1 Drain and weigh the fruit, reserving the syrup from the can. Arrange the fruit in a shallow heat-proof container.

2 Put the syrup in a measuring jug and add cold water to make up to 350ml (12fl oz). Weigh 225g (8oz) sugar and place this in a heavy saucepan with the syrup and water.

3 Over a gentle heat, and stirring constantly, bring the syrup to the boil. Pour it over the fruit to cover completely. Put a foil 'lid' over the dish, and set it aside for 24 hours.

4 Using a slotted spoon, carefully lift the fruit into a similar container and pour the syrup into a saucepan. Add a further 60g (2oz) sugar to the syrup and, stirring constantly, bring to the boil. Pour the syrup over the fruit, cover and set aside again for a further 24 hours.

Repeat step 4 twice more.

5 Lift the fruit from the syrup and pour the syrup into a saucepan with a further 90g (3oz) sugar. Stir the syrup constantly over a low heat until it *just* begins to boil. Remove from the heat and add the fruit to the pan. Return the pan to the heat and simmer gently for about three minutes. Carefully pour the syrup and fruit back into the dish. Cover again and leave to stand for 48 hours. After this time, check the consistency of the syrup. If it is thick and dense, cover the dish again, and leave the fruit for another 24

to 48 hours. If the syrup is still thin and runny, repeat step 5 once more.

6 When the fruit has stood in the thick syrup for at least three days (you may leave it a day or two longer if you wish), remove it from the dish and place it on a cooling rack. Stand the rack on a large tray to catch the dripping syrup. Allow the syrup to drain from the fruit for several hours, then place the rack over a baking tray or similar and place it in a *very cool* oven (the oven should be switched off before the fruit is placed inside) for one to two hours until the fruit is dry to touch. Take care not to allow the fruit to become hot, or the syrup will become toffee-like and will be spoiled.

7 To finish the fruit, pick up a piece at a time on the prongs of a fork, and dip it into boiling water. Shake to remove excess water, then dip the fruit in granulated sugar, turning to coat both sides. Remove from the sugar, and place on a cooling rack to dry thoroughly.

———————————————◆———————————————

FRESH FRUIT
Prepare the fruit and, if you are using fruit that would normally be cooked, cover with cold water, bring to the boil, and simmer until tender. Take care not to overcook. Proceed as for canned fruit (above), it will, however, be necessary to repeat step 4 and step 5 each once more.

◆ Glacé fruits ◆

To make glacé fruits, follow the same routine as for crystallized fruit (p. 57), but do not coat the fruits in granulated sugar to finish. Instead, use a thick sugar syrup as a final coat. This amount of syrup is suitable for about 450g (1lb) fruit.

340g (12oz) sugar
90ml (6tbsp) water

1 Make a strong sugar syrup by boiling the sugar with the water. Stir constantly until the sugar dissolves, then boil for one minute. Turn off the heat, and cover the syrup.

2 Take a little syrup at a time from the pan and put it in a small bowl, but keep the pan covered. As with crystallized fruit, dip each piece in boiling water, then in the syrup. Place on a rack to drain. Do not attempt to use the syrup once it becomes thick – this is why it is important to take only a little at a time from the pan. Take more syrup from the pan as necessary but do not add fresh syrup to syrup you have used – have a clean bowl each time.

Allow about 12 hours drying on the rack and turn the fruit at least once during this time.

◆ Crystallized peel ◆

This is an attractive and pleasant-tasting confection either as it is, with a complete chocolate coating, or with just chocolate 'tips'. Use whole fresh fruits with, as far as possible, unmarked skins. All citrus fruits give good results, but do not attempt to mix the peels in the same syrup or the individual flavours will be lost.

225g (8oz) prepared peel
280g (10oz) granulated sugar
caster sugar, for coating

1 Cut the fruits in half cross-wise. Scoop the flesh out of the shell, leaving the white pith and skin intact. Cut the peel into thick strips, cover with cold water, and leave overnight.

2 Drain the peel, place in a saucepan and cover with cold water. Bring to the boil, then drain. Repeat this process twice more.

3 Place the sugar in a large saucepan and then stir in 350ml (12fl oz) cold water. Stir constantly over a low heat until the sugar has dissolved. Bring the syrup to the boil, then add the peel.

4 Cook the peel in the syrup until it appears 'transparent'.

5 Remove the peel from the syrup using a slotted spoon and place on a wire rack to allow the syrup to drain off. Separate the pieces of peel and allow to dry for 48 hours.

6 Toss the pieces of peel in a shallow bowl of caster sugar. Store in an airtight container.

An impressive centrepiece for a buffet table, a bowl of frosted fruits is simple to prepare; small fruits like grapes (right) are best frosted in bunches. Crystallized pineapple, glacé pears and cherries, and marrons glacés are more time-consuming.

• Chocolate-covered candied peel •

Candied peel can be given attractive chocolate 'tips', or dipped in chocolate to cover completely. If you leave completely covered peel for a few days before eating, the sugar will produce a fruity-tasting liquid around the peel. Allow part-dipped peel to dry on parchment or polythene; completely coated strips are best left on a rack to dry.

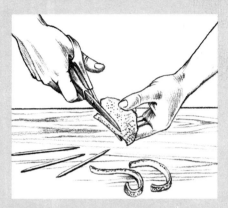

Follow the recipe for Crystallized peel, but omit step 6. Melt 115g (4oz) plain chocolate in a bowl over a pan of hot water, as described on p. 10. Cut the peel into strips, using scissors.

Dip each piece of peel in the chocolate to give a chocolate 'tip'. Or spear peel on a cocktail stick and dip in chocolate to coat completely. Remove the stick while the chocolate is still wet. Allow to dry.

• Frosted fruits •

Large or small fruits can be frosted and used in many different ways. Small, whole frosted fruits can be served in sweet cases or used to decorate cakes or desserts. It is also possible to frost whole large fruits such as apples, oranges or pears, and a 'fruit tower' using these looks spectacular as a centre piece for a dinner party or a buffet table. The following quantities will be sufficient to coat a small whole bunch of grapes and a good selection of medium-sized fruits to fill a fruit bowl or arrange in a display.

Small fruits, such as redcurrants, blackcurrants and small grapes are best left in little bunches, but should be washed and dried thoroughly. If you are using larger fruits, like apples or pears, try to choose firm fruits of similar size. Do not remove skin or peel, and wash and dry them thoroughly.

2 egg whites (or light sugar syrup, see below)
170g (6oz) caster sugar
prepared fruit
◆

1 If you are using egg whites, whisk them lightly. You can, if you prefer, use a light syrup made by mixing 60ml (4tbsp) icing sugar with 15–30ml (1–2tbsp) boiled water, but this will not give such a thick 'crust' to the fruit.

2 Place the caster sugar in a shallow dish or bowl.

3 For small fruits, dip each piece or small bunch of fruit in the egg white or syrup to coat. Shake gently to remove excess. Alternatively, drop the fruit into the sugar, turning to frost all sides. Set aside to dry.

4 For larger fruits, dip the fruits into egg white or syrup, or paint the egg white or syrup on to the surface of the fruit using a pastry brush.

5 Roll the fruits in the sugar, then sprinkle the sugar from a teaspoon on to the inaccessible areas. Set the fruits aside to dry.

• <u>Marrons glacés</u> •

A traditional Christmas treat for chestnut lovers, these can be prepared some time in advance as they keep well in an airtight container. Chestnuts are now available all year round – if you cannot obtain fresh chestnuts, you will get good results with canned or frozen ones. Even-sized fresh nuts are the best to use in my experience, since they are less likely to break up in the syrup.

MAKES ABOUT 675G (1½LB) FINISHED WEIGHT
about 675g (1½lb) fresh chestnuts in shells or about
450g (1lb) canned chestnuts (drained weight)
675g (1½lb) sugar
225g (8oz) powdered glucose
5ml (1tsp) vanilla essence

1 If you are using fresh chestnuts, prick the skins, then drop them into boiling water. Bring back to the boil and boil the nuts for 3–4 minutes. Drain the chestnuts and as soon as they are cool enough to handle, remove the shells and the dark skin. Place the chestnuts in a saucepan and cover with cold water. Bring to the boil and gently simmer until tender (about 8–10 minutes). Watch carefully – small nuts will be tender more quickly and will break up if you do not remove them from the pan at once.

2 Weigh 340g (12oz) of the sugar and put it, and the glucose and 2.5ml (½ tsp) of vanilla essence with 250ml (8fl oz) cold water into a large saucepan with a close-fitting lid (do not put the lid on at this stage).

3 Stir gently over a low heat until the sugar and glucose have dissolved. Test for undissolved sugar, as described on p. 44. Add the chestnuts and bring the pan to the boil.

4 Remove the pan from the heat. Put the lid on the saucepan and place it in a warm place for 48 hours.

5 Drain the chestnuts from the syrup. Make a fresh syrup with the remaining sugar and 140ml (5fl oz) water. Add 2.5ml (½tsp) vanilla essence. Stir over a gentle heat until the sugar has dissolved. Insert a sugar thermometer and continue to boil the syrup until it reaches a temperature of 120°C (250°F). Remove the pan from the heat, then add the chestnuts. Turn the nuts in the syrup to coat. Lift gently on to a wire rack to drain thoroughly. Leave on the rack until completely dry.

Store *marrons glacés* in an airtight container.

Fondants and Creams

Fondant is a soft, sweet delicate confection that usually has texture or flavour (or both) added to it, making it very versatile. It can be laced with liqueurs and used to fill chocolate cups and cases (see p. 23), flavoured with oils or essences and shaped into creams, which may or may not be dipped in chocolate, and wrapped round cherries before they are dipped in chocolate for a luxurious treat. There are several ways of making fondant – you can also buy it ready-made – and three basic recipes are included here, all of which can be modified and used in many ways to give an array of shapes and flavours that will add interest and variation to any chocolate assortment.

• Making fondant •

There are several different ways of making fondant. A cooked fondant is probably the cheapest, but it is the most difficult to master at first. Also, it is advisable, if not essential, to have a sugar thermometer for the cooking process, as you must be sure that the sugar syrup reaches the correct temperature. Alternatively, a simple and delicious fondant can be made with lightly whisked egg whites and icing sugar. This is much easier to get right first time. Similarly, a simple, soft-textured fondant is easily produced with sweetened condensed milk and icing sugar. It is also possible to buy a ready-made type of fondant icing from many shops and supermarkets.

It is important to remember that any fondant to be used in chocolate centres must be made well in advance so that it is set before you use it. Fondant keeps very well so this should not present any problems. It will become quite firm, even hard, with keeping, but this does not really matter too much as fondant is very well behaved when warmed or melted over hot water, like chocolate. Again like chocolate, it is most important not to let fondant overheat as it will ruin the texture. As it does keep so well, it is a good idea to make plenty of fondant at one time. Any that is not used can simply be wrapped and kept for next time. This applies particularly to cooked fondant as it is quite a long process that requires patience to complete, and it is possible to flavour, colour and add to fondant in so many ways that you can make lots of different chocolate centres from one basic recipe.

A marble slab, if you have one, can be useful when you are fondant-making. You can manage quite well without one, however – a baking sheet or metal tea-tray also makes a good surface to work on. Chill either in the top of your freezer for an hour or so beforehand and you will get excellent results. If you are using a tray it is probably best to set it on a damp towel on a worktop, to stop the tray from skidding about while you are working the fondant.

Peppermint creams, lightly coloured green and part and wholly dipped in chocolate,
with, in the foreground, a basket of fondant creams, decorated with contrasting chocolate.

• Cooked creamy fondant •

A creamy fondant is a good base for a variety of chocolate centres, and will keep for a long time. Making a cooked fondant is an exacting process, so be sure to make plenty and just wrap and keep what you do not need at once. When stored, fondant tends to harden but, if you warm it gently in a bowl over hot water, it will soon become soft and creamy again.

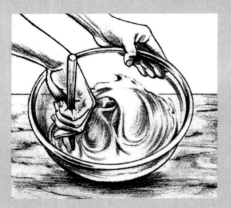

Work the cooked fondant in a figure eight movement in a dampened bowl. It will become difficult to work with as it sets, and be stiff and white in appearance and crumbly in texture.

Turn the fondant on to a dampened cold surface and knead it to bind together. Continue to knead until the fondant is smooth and pliable (about 15–20 minutes). This is quite hard work.

• Cooked fondant •

This recipe will make a little less than 450g (1lb) finished weight fondant. If you want more than this, simply use the same recipe but double or treble the quantities, as necessary. If you have more than this amount, however, it may be difficult to work the syrup in a bowl before kneading it. If so, turn the fondant on to your dampened marble slab or chilled tray and work the 'figure eight' with a scraper or spatula. It will start off as a sticky, fluid mass, and should be allowed to cool slightly before you start.

MAKES ABOUT 450G (1LB)
450g (1lb) granulated sugar
150ml (5fl oz) water
25ml (5tsp) liquid glucose
———◆———

1 Place your cooking thermometer in a jug of hot water.

2 In a large, heavy-based saucepan, combine the water and sugar. Stir with a wooden spoon over a low heat until the sugar is dissolved. If any crystals of undissolved sugar remain on the side of the pan, brush them down into the syrup with a pastry brush dipped in cold water. Test for undissolved sugar, as described on p. 44.

3 When the sugar has dissolved, stir in the liquid glucose and place your thermometer in the syrup. Bring the syrup to the boil and boil steadily until the temperature reaches 115–116°C (239–240°F).

4 Immediately remove the pan from the heat and plunge the base in a bowl of cold water to arrest the cooking process. Remove the thermometer. Stir for a moment or two, then pour the syrup carefully into a large, heat-proof bowl which has been rinsed in cold water and left just damp. Allow the syrup to rest for a minute before working and kneading, as described opposite.

5 When the fondant has become smooth and putty-like, wrap it first in cling film, then in kitchen foil, and leave it in a cool place for at least 24 hours before use.

◆ Uncooked fondant ◆

Uncooked fondant will not keep as long as cooked fondant, so make it in small quantities that you will be able to use up. It also behaves slightly differently in use – you may, for instance, find you have to leave finished sweets in a warm place for several hours to dry out the surface. The taste and texture, though, are very good.

MAKES ABOUT 450G (1LB)
450g (1lb) icing sugar, sifted
1 large egg white
15–30ml (1–2tbsp) liquid glucose

◆

1 In a large bowl, lightly beat the egg white until just frothy. Add the icing sugar in thirds, beating well. As the fondant becomes too thick to mix, add a little liquid glucose. Take care not to add too much – you are aiming to produce a firm, white, smooth mixture which is pliable but not sticky. If the fondant does become sticky, add more icing sugar.

2 Remove from the bowl and knead lightly on a surface lightly dusted with icing sugar.

3 Wrap the fondant and chill for at least three to four hours before use.

◆ Uncooked creamy fondant ◆

With this recipe, again only make what you can reasonably use up. This is a more sticky fondant, but it is very pleasant to eat and simple to make. It may require up to two days' chilling before it will hold its shape. Once it has been cut into shapes, you may have to chill the fondant again before dipping, but you will find that you get good results if you do not try to rush it.

MAKES ABOUT 450G (1LB)
450g (1lb) icing sugar, sifted
200g (7oz) sweetened condensed milk

◆

65

1 Place the icing sugar in a large bowl. Add the condensed milk, a spoonful at a time, mixing well after each addition. Do not add too much milk.

2 Remove the mixture from the bowl and knead on a surface lightly dusted with icing sugar. The fondant should be soft and pliable at this stage, but hold its shape.

3 Wrap the fondant in cling film and chill for at least an hour, or until very firm, before use.

• Chocolate-dipped fondant cherries •

These delicious little chocolates are always a show-stopper if you can manage to obtain maraschino cherries with the stalks still attached. It is important that the cherries are *completely* dry before you dip them into the fondant.

MAKES ABOUT 30 FONDANT CHERRIES
225g (8oz) jar maraschino cherries, stalks attached if possible
225g (8oz) fondant
340g (12oz) plain chocolate
115g (4oz) chocolate vermicelli

1 Drain the cherries and dry them well on absorbent paper.

2 Gently melt the fondant in a bowl over a pan of hot water. Do not allow it to become hot, it should be thick and syrupy. Remove the bowl from the pan.

3 Place a sheet of baking parchment on a tray. Dip the cherries one by one in the fondant, then place on the parchment to set. If you are using cherries with stalks attached, take care that the fondant does not cover the stalk, but leave a little space around the stem. Cherries without stems are easy to coat using a dipping ring.

4 When the fondant around the cherries is firm and set, line a second tray with parchment or polythene.

5 Melt the chocolate in a bowl over a pan of hot water, as described on p. 10. Remove the bowl from the pan and allow the chocolate to cool slightly before dipping the cherries to coat them completely with the chocolate. Stand the cherries on the second tray to dry.

6 Shake the chocolate vermicelli in a shallow layer on a large baking tray.

7 When the first coating of chocolate is set and hard, dip the cherries again to give a second complete coating. Gently shake off any excess, and stand the cherries on the layer of vermicelli, to give a flat 'foot' for the cherries to stand on when dry.

These cherries will improve with two or three days' keeping.

• Pineapple fondant cups •

This is another delightful chocolate centre with a fondant base. The tiny pieces of fruit inside the chocolate cups are a succulent surprise. It is far better to use tinned pineapple than fresh for this type of centre, but don't use those brands canned in syrup – the sweetness of the fondant is complemented by a more natural fruit taste.

Maraschino cherries, their stalks still attached, wrapped in fondant, then dipped in chocolate. The cherries form their own liqueur if made a few days before being eaten.

67

TO FILL 25–30 CUPS
115g (4oz) pineapple pieces, in natural juice
45ml (3tbsp) pineapple liqueur
170g (6oz) fondant
chocolate cups (see p. 23)

◆

1 Drain the pineapple and chop finely. Place in a shallow dish and pour over the liqueur. Allow to stand for at least three hours, or overnight if possible.

2 Warm the fondant in a bowl over a pan of hot water. When the fondant is runny and smooth, remove the bowl from the pan. Stir the fondant off the heat for about one minute.

3 Add the pineapple and liqueur to the fondant, stirring well to mix. Set aside to cool completely.

4 Fill the cups with the fondant mixture. Chill the open cups until the mixture is firm before adding the lids. Be sure that the edges of the lids are well sealed.

◆

VARIATIONS
You could also use blackcurrants (do not chop them) with crème de cassis, and mandarin oranges with grand marnier for this recipe.

◆ Cream eggs ◆

A very popular treat for children, Easter eggs with a fondant 'cream' filling are time-consuming, but not difficult, to make. A mould that will produce finished eggs the size of small hen's eggs is perfect, but you can use any mould, as long as it is not too big. A really large egg with a soft filling will break when you unmould it. If you wish to change the taste of the egg, flavour the fondant with a hint of mint, coffee or orange, but avoid a very strong flavour in a confection of this kind where there is so much fondant in relation to chocolate.

MAKES 6–8 SMALL/MEDIUM-SIZED EGGS
340–400g (12–14oz) chocolate
225–340g (8–12oz) fondant
yellow food colouring

◆

1 Make hollow egg shells in the moulds using 225–285g (8–10oz) of chocolate, as described on p. 16. Leave them in the moulds.

2 Have all the fondant at room temperature. Colour 60g (2oz) yellow.

3 Fill each half-egg to within 6mm (¼in) of the rim with white fondant. Place 5g (1tsp) of yellow fondant on top of the white. Chill until firm. Meanwhile melt the remaining 115g (4oz) chocolate and allow to cool but not set.

4 When the fondant is firm to the touch, remove the half-eggs from the refrigerator. Carefully spoon the melted chocolate over the fondant. The chocolate should come almost to the rim of the egg. Chill again until the chocolate is set.

5 Remove the completed eggs from the moulds and sandwich two halves together by running a little melted chocolate round the rims, or by dabbing dots of melted chocolate over the egg halves and pressing them gently together.

• Peppermint creams •

These soft and delicate little sweets are a traditional favourite which many people enjoy as a sweet treat or after a meal. The rich, creamy fondant this recipe gives needs several hours to dry out before serving.

MAKES ABOUT 450G (1LB)
1 egg white
45ml (3tbsp) double cream
a few drops of peppermint oil
a few drops of green food colouring (optional)
approx 450g (1lb) icing sugar, sifted

1 In a large bowl, whisk the egg white until frothy. Add the cream and a little peppermint oil and stir well. If you wish to add a little green food colouring, it will be easier to do so now, but take care not to add too much.

2 Add the icing sugar, a little at a time, mixing it in with a metal spoon at first, then kneading by hand as the mixture becomes firm. Continue to add the icing sugar until the fondant is fairly stiff, but not dry.

3 Wrap the fondant in cling film and leave for about one hour to rest.

4 Dust a work surface liberally with icing sugar and place the fondant on it. Using an icing-sugar-dusted rolling pin, roll out the fondant to about 6mm (¼in) thick and cut out shapes using petits fours cutters.

5 Place the peppermint creams on a sheet of baking parchment to dry. This will take about 8–12 hours. Turn the sweets at least once during drying.

VARIATIONS
Green and white creams Try leaving half the mixture white and colouring half very pale green. To do this, break the finished fondant in two before resting it, and knead a few drops of colouring evenly through it.

Chocolate-dipped peppermint creams Use plain 25mm (1in) round cutters and, when the fondant is dry, dip the sweets in chocolate to cover one half only. Alternatively, drizzle chocolate lines over the top of the creams.

• Fondant creams •

One recipe of fondant will give you enough to try a variety of flavours, which can also be coated in chocolate or left as they are. Make a selection, identifying each type with a different marking or topping, after you have dipped them in chocolate (as described on p. 43). Candied petals (see p. 88) make a lovely finishing touch for violet and rose creams, in particular, whether they are chocolate-coated or not. Serve in sweet cases.

Coffee or orange creams Knead a few drops of coffee essence or a little orange oil, and a little brown or orange food colouring into the fondant recipe.

Lemon, rose, and violet creams You might have to search for these flavours as they are a little difficult to come by, but they are well worth trying.

Almond, raspberry, and strawberry creams Almond creams are subtle and delicious, and children love the flavour of strawberry and raspberry. Strawberry and raspberry creams can also be coloured, as appropriate.

Chocolate Truffles

Chocolate truffles are a delicious mixture of chocolate and dairy products – butter, milk, and cream – which can be varied in many ways. They can be made rich and creamy, or firm and chocolatey, laced with liqueurs for adults, or made with cake crumbs for a children's party. They can be made from milk, plain, or white chocolate, and finished in almost any shape or colour you choose. These many variations make truffles a favourite for home chocolate-making. Included in this section are recipes and suggestions for finishes for truffles. You may like to experiment with different finishes, however, so I have included some ideas at the end of the chapter. The suggestions with the recipes are for what I think suit a particular truffle, either for easy identification or to complement or contrast with what is in the centre. There are no hard and fast 'rules' so don't be afraid to try something different.

· Making chocolate truffles ·

There are many variations on the following three basic recipes, some of which are detailed after the individual recipes. One thing to remember is that the addition of the dry ingredients, like nuts, makes the truffle mixture much easier to handle when you are rolling it into balls. It might, therefore, be better to attempt some of the truffles with dry ingredients first. The really 'wet' mixes – those with sherry or champagne, for example – are more difficult at the rolling stage. If you find it difficult forming the mixture into balls with a teaspoon and your hands, as shown on p. 72, try one of the following suggestions. Whichever method you choose, remember that the mixture will quickly become very soft again once it is removed from the refrigerator so when dipping only take a few at a time to keep the rest firm enough to hold their shape.

METHOD ONE
Divide the mixture into four portions. Dust a flat surface with plenty of icing sugar, then roll each portion into a sausage shape. Chill for about 30 minutes in the refrigerator, then cut each sausage shape into slices about 12–19mm (½–¾in) wide. Roll each slice into a ball. Chill again for about an hour before dipping in chocolate.

METHOD TWO
A really soft mixture might be better spooned into a piping bag fitted with a large plain nozzle. Squeeze walnut-sized blobs on to a sheet of baking parchment. Chill the mixture until firm, then roll the blobs into balls.

An assortment of chocolate truffles, dipped in milk and plain chocolate, then finished with caster sugar, milk and plain chocolate vermicelli, chopped nuts, sifted icing sugar and cocoa powder, and contrasting chocolate markings.

⋅ Truffle techniques ⋅

A basic truffle is so versatile that, once the technique is mastered, it opens a whole range to the home chocolate-maker. It is important to pay careful attention to the temperatures of the ingredients at all stages. Cool the melted chocolate, but not so much that it begins to set. Soften the butter, but do not let it become liquid. Leave the finished mixture to become firm, but do not allow it to set hard. Each of the stages involved in truffle-making is as important as the others, and you must recognize when the mixture is 'right' at every stage – it may take one or two attempts but each time you try, every stage will become more obvious.

Add the softened butter, a little at a time, to the melted and cooled chocolate, mixing well after each addition.

Use a little icing sugar to prevent the mixture sticking to your hands while you roll it into balls.

Place the truffles on a greaseproof sheet and, if necessary, chill again until they are firm enough to dip.

You may find it helpful to have a fork ready to help roll the dipped truffle in your chosen finish to coat completely.

• Traditional rum truffles •

Rich and dark, these truffles are a Christmas favourite but they also make delicious after-dinner treats on their own or with a selection of other truffles, and are an acceptable addition to a gift box of home-made chocolates.

MAKES ABOUT 30 TRUFFLES
340g (12oz) plain chocolate
30ml (2tbsp) cool, strong black coffee
115g (4oz) unsalted butter, softened
30ml (2tbsp) dark rum
a little icing sugar, sifted
chocolate vermicelli, to finish

1 Break 225g (8oz) of the chocolate into small pieces and place it in a heat-proof bowl with the coffee. Melt the chocolate over a pan of hot, but not boiling water, as described on p. 10. Do not allow the bottom of the bowl to touch the water. Stir gently until the chocolate has completely melted.

2 Remove the bowl from the pan and continue to stir the chocolate until it begins to cool and thicken slightly.

3 Add the butter, as shown opposite, and the rum, a little at a time. Cover and chill the mixture until it is firm enough to handle (about one hour).

4 Dust your hands lightly with the icing sugar. Using a teaspoon and your hands, form the mixture into walnut-sized balls. Chill again.

5 Melt the remaining 115g (4oz) chocolate as before. Remove the bowl from the pan. The chocolate should be fluid, but cool.

6 Dip each truffle quickly in the chocolate and roll immediately in the vermicelli before the outside coating begins to dry.

Serve in paper sweet cases.

VARIATIONS
This recipe can be varied by omitting the rum and coffee and adding instead any of these liqueurs: cognac; apricot brandy; benedictine; cointreau; drambuie; tia maria; or port. With all of them, 30–45ml (2–3tbsp) will normally be sufficient, depending on your taste, but it is possible to add up to 60ml (4tbsp) of liquid without difficulty.

If you would rather have non-alcoholic truffles, either omit the rum and double the amount of coffee in the basic recipe, or omit both rum and coffee, and add instead: a few drops of peppermint oil or essence; a few drops of orange oil or essence; 90g (3oz) chopped hazelnuts or walnuts; or 15ml (1tbsp) minced ginger mixed with 30ml (2tbsp) milk.

• White chocolate truffles •

Not everyone enjoys the flavour of alcohol in confectionery. By mixing white chocolate with cream, you will produce a delicate texture and subtle flavour. White chocolate is not as easy to work with as milk or plain chocolate as it burns easily, so although the chocolate should be melted completely, it must never be allowed to overheat. The creamy taste and attractive appearance of white chocolates make the extra effort worth while.

MAKES ABOUT 20–25 TRUFFLES
225g (8oz) white chocolate
60g (2oz) unsalted butter, softened
45ml (3tbsp) single cream
a little icing sugar, sifted
desiccated coconut, to finish

1 Break the chocolate into small pieces and melt gently in a heat-proof bowl over a pan of hot, but not boiling water, as described on p. 10. Take special care not to allow the chocolate to become hot, but just melted.

2 Immediately remove the bowl from the pan and stir the chocolate for a minute or two until the outside of the bowl feels cool.

3 Gradually stir in the butter. Slowly add the cream, pouring it in a thin stream and folding it into the chocolate. Cover and chill the mixture until it is firm enough to handle.

4 Dust your hands lightly with icing sugar. Using a teaspoon and your hands, form the mixture into small balls, as shown on p. 72. Roll the truffles in the coconut to coat them completely.

Serve in paper sweet cases.

VARIATIONS
Try using the white chocolate truffle with any of the following variations: 60ml (4tbsp) cherry brandy, and a few drops of pink food colouring; 90ml (6tbsp) sloe gin; 60ml (4tbsp) malibu; or 60ml (4tbsp) whisky.

For a non-alcoholic white chocolate truffle, add 90g (3oz) chopped almonds, and a few drops of almond essence to the basic recipe.

◆ Rich milk chocolate truffles ◆

Milk chocolate produces a light and creamy texture but you could substitute plain chocolate to make a slightly less sweet truffle. Alternatively, roll the finished truffles in cocoa powder only to reduce the sweetness.

MAKES ABOUT 25 TRUFFLES
340g (12oz) milk chocolate
60g (2oz) unsalted butter, softened
45ml (3tbsp) unsweetened evaporated milk
30g (1oz) cocoa powder
30g (1oz) icing sugar

1 Break 225g (8oz) of the chocolate into small pieces and melt gently in a heat-proof bowl over a pan of hot, but not boiling water, as described on p. 10. Take care not to allow the chocolate to become hot, but just melted.

2 Remove the bowl from the pan and stir the chocolate for a minute or two until the outside of the bowl feels cool.

3 Gradually add the butter, incorporating each addition thoroughly. Slowly pour in the evaporated milk,

White chocolate truffles, finished with chocolate markings, chopped roasted nuts, coconut, and granulated sugar. A mix of milk and white chocolate gives a distinctive appearance.

folding it into the chocolate mixture. Cover and chill the mixture until it is firm enough to handle (about one hour).

4 Sieve together the cocoa powder and icing sugar.

5 Melt the remaining 115g (4oz) chocolate as before. Remove the bowl from the pan. Dust your hands lightly with icing sugar. Using a teaspoon and your hands, form the mixture into small balls, as shown on p. 72.

6 With a dipping ring, dip each truffle in the chocolate and roll immediately in the combined cocoa powder and icing sugar. Allow the truffles to dry for a few moments before lifting them.

Serve in paper sweet cases.

◆

VARIATIONS

This basic recipe can be varied with the addition of any of the following: 90ml (6tbsp) Bailey's Irish cream liqueur; 60ml (4tbsp) amaretto, and a few drops of almond essence; 90ml (6tbsp) sherry; 60ml (4tbsp) grand marnier; or 90ml (6tbsp) kirsch.

For a non-alcoholic milk chocolate truffle, add 45ml (3tbsp) clear honey, slightly warmed.

◆ Champagne truffles ◆

The taste of champagne is very difficult to transfer from the bottle into chocolates. However, the addition of real champagne or sparkling wine will produce a light and delicate texture that nothing else quite matches. Be very careful when adding so much fluid to the chocolate mixture. It must be done very gradually. If the mixture starts to separate or curdle, do not attempt to add any more liquid; it will still be usable as long as you do not add more liquid. Immediately stop stirring and put the mixture in a cool place until it is almost set. Stir again very gently, then leave to set completely before handling the mixture further.

It is most important that the chocolate should be melted and *thoroughly cooled* for this recipe. The addition of the butter to the cooled chocolate is a little more difficult and the resulting ganache is thicker and creamier than in the other truffle recipes. If you do not start with a thick creamy mixture, however, it will be impossible to add fluid.

MAKES ABOUT 35–40 TRUFFLES
340g (12oz) milk chocolate
115g (4oz) unsalted butter, diced and slightly softened
150ml (5fl oz) champagne, sparkling wine, or champagne perry
115g (4oz) white chocolate, to coat
◆

1 Break the chocolate into small pieces and melt in a heat-proof bowl over a pan of hot, but not boiling water, as described on p. 10. Stir gently until the chocolate is just melted.

2 Immediately remove the bowl from the pan and leave the chocolate to cool.

3 Stir the chocolate thoroughly, then gradually add the butter. The mixture should be thick and creamy and slightly grainy in appearance.

4 Slowly add the champagne, stirring gently. Do not beat the mixture. Cover and leave to set. This may take two to three hours.

5 Dust your hands lightly with icing sugar. Using a teaspoon and your hands, mould the mixture into small balls. Chill the truffles until firm.

6 Melt the white chocolate as before. Remove the bowl from the pan and allow to cool slightly.

7 Dip your fingers into the chocolate and coat the truffles one at a time by rolling them in your chocolate-coated hands. Place the finished truffles on a sheet of heavy-gauge polythene to set. Serve in paper sweet cases.

• Chocolate truffles •

An economical recipe. Less rich, and with no alcohol content, these truffles are ideal for children. You could substitute drinking chocolate for the cocoa powder to make them even more acceptable to younger people.

MAKES ABOUT 25 TRUFFLES
115g (4oz) unsalted butter, softened
90g (3oz) icing sugar, sifted
115g (4oz) plain chocolate
170g (6oz) fine cake crumbs (Madeira or any plain cake)
cocoa powder, to finish

———◆———

1 In a large bowl, cream together the butter and icing sugar.
2 Break the chocolate into small pieces and melt in a heat-proof bowl over a pan of hot water, as described on p. 10. Cool slightly, then add the chocolate to the butter mixture, stirring as you do so.
3 Gradually add the cake crumbs and mix thoroughly.

4 Dust your hands lightly with icing sugar. Using a teaspoon and your hands, form the mixture into walnut-sized balls as shown on p. 72, and roll them in the cocoa powder so that they are completely coated.
5 Leave the truffles in a cool place until they become firm.
Serve in paper sweet cases.

• Vanilla truffles •

A mixture of white and milk chocolate gives these truffles an attractive and distinctive appearance and taste. Do not be tempted to add a greater proportion of milk chocolate, however, as the delicate balance of colour will be lost.

MAKES ABOUT 30 TRUFFLES
225g (8oz) white chocolate
140g (5oz) milk chocolate
90g (3oz) unsalted butter, softened
45ml (3tbsp) unsweetened evaporated milk
5ml (1tsp) vanilla essence

———◆———

1 Break 115g (4oz) white chocolate and 115g (4oz) milk chocolate into small pieces and melt gently in a heat-proof bowl over a pan of hot, but not boiling water, as described on p. 10.
2 Remove the bowl from the pan.

Stir the chocolate well to combine, then allow to cool slightly.
3 Gradually stir in the butter. When all the butter is incorporated, pour in the evaporated milk in a thin stream, folding it into the chocolate.

4 Add the vanilla essence a few drops at a time and taste the mixture between additions. When you are happy with the vanilla flavour, cover the mixture and allow to set.

5 Melt the remaining chocolate as before. Remove the bowl from the pan and stir the chocolate well.

6 Dust your hands lightly with icing sugar. Using a teaspoon and your hands, form the mixture into small balls, as shown on p. 72. Dip each truffle in the chocolate, then place them on a sheet of heavy-gauge polythene until the chocolate is set.

Serve in paper sweet cases.

• Strawberry truffles •

Fruit truffles are fresher and cleaner-tasting than other kinds of chocolate truffles, and the addition of chopped fruit or fruit essences in the recipes that follow is a pleasant change from the flavours of alcohol more usually associated with chocolate truffles. Like some of the other less common fruit essences, natural strawberry essence can be difficult to find. Search for it in specialist confectioners' shops – these rich and creamy truffles are worth the effort involved.

MAKES ABOUT 20–25 TRUFFLES
315g (11oz) white chocolate
a few drops of natural strawberry essence
a few drops of pink food colouring
45ml (3tbsp) single cream
60g (2oz) unsalted butter, softened
a little icing sugar, sifted
115g (4oz) pink coloured sugar (see p. 84), to finish

1 Break 225g (8oz) of the chocolate into small pieces and melt gently in a heat-proof bowl over a pan of hot, but not boiling water, as described on p. 10. Take special care not to allow the chocolate to become hot, but just melted.

2 Remove the bowl from the pan and stir the chocolate until it begins to cool but not set.

3 Add about 2.5ml (½tsp) strawberry essence and about the same amount of pink food colouring to the cream. Stir gently and set aside.

4 Gradually stir the butter into the chocolate mixture. Slowly add the cream, pouring it in a thin stream and folding it into the chocolate. Cover and chill the mixture until it is firm enough to handle.

5 Dust your hands lightly with icing sugar. Using a teaspoon and your hands, roll the mixture into small balls, as shown on p. 72. Place the truffles on a tray covered with greaseproof paper and chill them in the refrigerator for about an hour.

6 Melt the remaining 90g (3oz) chocolate as before. Remove the bowl from the pan and allow to cool, stirring occasionally.

7 Shake the coloured sugar in a layer into a shallow dish. Have a tablespoon in the dish.

8 Using a dipping ring, dip each truffle quickly in the chocolate, then drop it into the sugar. With the tablespoon, cover the truffle with the sugar, turning it

Fruit truffles make a refreshing change from the more usual flavours. The selection here includes orange, strawberry, lemon and lime truffles, all finished with coloured sugar.

to ensure no area is missed. Allow the truffles to dry before lifting them out of the sugar-covered dish.

Serve in white sweet cases.

VARIATIONS

Raspberry truffles Use the same recipe as for strawberry truffles but replace the strawberry essence with raspberry. Make the coloured sugar for raspberry truffles with scarlet food colouring. It will still only appear dark pink, but will be enough to identify raspberry sugar from the strawberry.

Orange or lemon truffles Use the strawberry truffle recipe but change the essence and colour for orange or lemon essence, and a little appropriate colouring. The addition of finely grated rind of orange or lemon can be made, if you wish, after the cream. However, do not be tempted to include the juice of the fruit as this may make the truffle mixture separate and will inhibit the setting of the chocolates.

• Rum and raisin truffles •

If you wish, you can use fruit juice instead of rum, or substitute sherry or brandy for a change of flavour. Whatever you choose to use, it is a good idea to soak the raisins for a while to make them plump and concentrate the flavour of the fruit juice or liqueur.

MAKES ABOUT 25–30 TRUFFLES
115g (4oz) seedless raisins
60ml (4tbsp) dark rum
140g (5oz) plain chocolate
115g (4oz) unsalted butter, softened
115g (4oz) ground almonds
115g (4oz) icing sugar, sifted
cocoa powder or vermicelli, to finish

1 Place the raisins in a small bowl. Pour over the rum and stir. Cover and leave to stand for about an hour.

2 Break the chocolate into small pieces and melt gently in a heat-proof bowl over a pan of hot, but not boiling water, as described on p. 10.

3 Remove the bowl from the pan and allow the chocolate to cool.

4 Add the butter a little at a time, and stir well. Stir in the ground almonds and icing sugar, then the rum and raisins.

Mix well, cover and allow the mixture to stand until it is firm enough to handle. Chill if necessary.

5 Dust your hands lightly with icing sugar. Using a teaspoon and your hands, form the mixture into small balls, as shown on p. 72. Roll the truffles in the cocoa powder or vermicelli so that they are completely coated. Lift the truffles, place them gently on a tray and chill again until firm.

Serve in paper sweet cases.

• Apricot truffles •

You can substitute almost any dried fruits for the apricots in this recipe with equal success, so long as they are finely chopped. A food processor, if you have one, is very handy for this job.

MAKES ABOUT 30 TRUFFLES
115g (4oz) white chocolate
15ml (1tbsp) sweetened condensed milk
15ml (1tbsp) apricot jam, sieved
115g (4oz) dried apricots, finely chopped
60g (2oz) ground almonds
60g (2oz) icing sugar, sifted
90g (3oz) sweetened desiccated coconut, to finish

1 Break the chocolate into small pieces and melt carefully in a heat-proof bowl over a pan of hot, but not boiling water, as described on p. 10.

2 Remove the bowl from the pan and allow the chocolate to cool.

3 Carefully stir in the condensed milk and jam, then add the apricots and ground almonds, and finally the icing sugar. Mix well, cover and chill the mixture until it is firm enough to handle.

4 Dust your hands lightly with icing sugar. Using a teaspoon and your hands, form the mixture into small balls, as shown on p. 72. Roll the truffles in the coconut to coat them completely, then chill again if necessary.

Serve in paper sweet cases.

◆ Cherry truffles ◆

A change from all-chocolate truffles, a cherry centre is simple to produce. If the cherries have a lot of syrup round them, wash and dry them thoroughly on absorbent kitchen paper. This will make it easier to mould the mixture round the cherries.

MAKES ABOUT 30 TRUFFLES
60g (2oz) plain chocolate
115g (4oz) fine cake crumbs (Madeira or any plain cake)
60g (2oz) ground almonds
60g (2oz) icing sugar, sifted
60ml (4tbsp) apricot jam, sieved
approx 60ml (4tbsp) sweetened condensed milk
30 glacé cherries, whole
115g (4oz) milk chocolate
a few glacé cherries, roughly chopped, to finish

1 Break the plain chocolate into small pieces and melt carefully in a heat-proof bowl over a pan of hot, but not boiling water, as described on p. 10.

2 Remove the bowl from the pan and stir in the cake crumbs and ground almonds. Add the icing sugar and jam, and enough condensed milk to give a firm but stiff mixture which will be sticky at this stage. Chill the mixture briefly (about 10 minutes).

3 Dust your hands lightly with icing sugar. Mould about a teaspoon of the mixture around a cherry. Place the truffles on a tray and chill until very firm.

4 Melt the milk chocolate. Remove the bowl from the pan and allow to cool.

5 Dip each truffle into the chocolate, and place it on a sheet of polythene. Top each truffle with a piece of glacé cherry before the chocolate is dry.

Serve in paper sweet cases.

⋅ Almond praline ⋅

The term 'praline' is used for two different types of confection. In Europe, it is usually used to refer to a type of nutty paste or soft nougatine which, when added to chocolate, gives a soft and creamy texture but retains the nutty flavour. This soft praline is made using very complicated machinery, and is impossible to make at home; although you can sometimes buy it from specialist confectionery suppliers, in my experience it is difficult to obtain in small quantities.

In the UK and USA, praline is more commonly a crunchy sweetmeat made of nuts and brittle caramel. This is easy to make and can either be eaten as it is, or crushed and used in a variety of ways. It is a delicious addition to ice-cream, and can be included in recipes for cakes and biscuits for variety; it also gives a pleasant taste and texture to chocolate truffles. Finish praline truffles by rolling them in crushed almonds or hazelnuts. You can use almost any nuts you choose in praline. They need not be whole since most recipes using praline call for it to be crushed anyway.

MAKES ABOUT 340G (12OZ)
225g (8oz) whole blanched almonds
225g (8oz) granulated sugar
45ml (3tbsp) water

1 Preheat the oven to 180°C/350°F/gas mark 4.

2 Spread the almonds evenly on a baking tray and 'toast' them in the oven for about five to six minutes, until browned. Meanwhile, oil a marble slab or large baking sheet.

3 Combine the sugar and water in a heavy-based saucepan and, using a wooden spoon, stir over a medium-low heat until the sugar has dissolved. Test for undissolved sugar, as described on p. 44. Bring to the boil. Continue to boil, without stirring, until the syrup turns a pale golden colour.

4 Remove the pan from the heat and stir in the warm nuts.

5 Turn the praline on to the prepared marble slab or baking sheet and leave to set.

6 The easiest way to crush the praline is to pound it with a wooden mallet or rolling pin. Alternatively, grind it in a food processor.

⋅ Chocolate praline squares ⋅

These squares can be dipped in chocolate or eaten as they are. If you are going to dip them, remember to cut them quite small since this is such a rich sweet. You could make a 'chocolate sandwich' from this recipe by spreading a layer of chocolate about 6mm (¼in) thick in the bottom of the lined tin and allowing it to set firm before adding the praline mixture. Allow to set, then top with more melted chocolate. Mark into squares before the top coating of chocolate sets hard.

MAKES ABOUT 25–30 SQUARES
225g (8oz) plain chocolate
60g (2oz) unsalted butter, diced
170g (6oz) crushed praline

1 Line a 15cm (6in) or 18cm (7in) square baking tin with non-stick baking parchment.

2 Melt the chocolate in a heat-proof bowl over a pan of hot water, as described on p. 10. Remove from the heat, allow the chocolate to cool slightly, then gradually add the butter. Mix well. Add the praline and stir thoroughly to combine.

3 Turn into the prepared tin and leave to set in a cool place. When cold and firm, remove from the tin and cut into squares.

• Finishes •

As in all forms of food preparation, the finishing touch is very important in chocolates and truffles. The finish can sometimes help to identify the flavour or content of a chocolate, but an array of different chocolates always looks interesting. If a truffle centre is first dipped in melted chocolate, it is possible to roll it in many different textures to change the appearance or colour of the chocolate.

Remember also that if the truffle centre is made with plain chocolate, the outside coating does not necessarily have to be dark too. Try dipping a white-centred truffle in dark chocolate, then rolling it in sifted icing sugar. The resulting white-dark-white when the truffle is bitten into is quite a surprise.

• Chopped and roasted nuts •

Nuts are versatile enough to be included in the truffle centre and, when chopped and toasted, make an attractive and appealing finish.

Almonds and hazelnuts should have the skins removed before you use them. Blanch almonds by placing them in a saucepan of cold water. Bring quickly to the boil and remove from the heat. Remove one almond and squeeze it gently between your thumb and index finger. The nut should pop out of the skin quite readily. If it does not, return the pan to the heat, but do not *cook* the nuts. Drain and rinse the nuts in cold water. Remove the skins and place the nuts on absorbent paper. Be sure the nuts are dry before you use them.

To remove the skins from hazelnuts, spread them evenly on a baking sheet, and put them in an oven preheated to 180°C/350°F/gas mark 4 for 10–12 minutes until the skins are dry and flaking. Remove the nuts from the oven and allow to cool for a minute or two. You should now be able to rub off the skins using a dry tea-towel.

⋄ Colouring sugar ⋄

Coloured sugar can be a useful way of finishing truffles or decorating white chocolates. Use pink or red colouring for raspberry or strawberry, orange or brown for tangerine or coffee, and green for lime and mint. Start with a little sugar only – this will take on quite a strong colour. Add increasing amounts of sugar to dilute the strength of colour, and stop adding sugar when it reaches the shade you want.

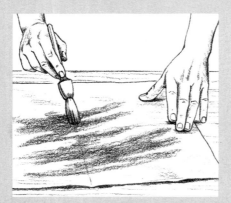

Line a swiss-roll tin with greaseproof paper and paint the paper lightly with food colouring.

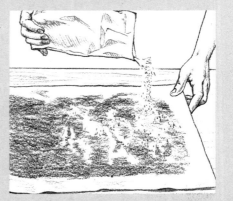

Sprinkle caster sugar over the paper. Start with a small amount of sugar, you can always add more later.

Draw one end of the paper up over the sugar and level with the opposite end, so that the sugar is enveloped inside. Then, pressing lightly with the palm of your hand, work the sugar to and fro inside the paper.

As with all finishing ingredients, it is best to have more than you need, rather than not enough. If you do find that you have more than you require immediately, store it in an airtight jar. Coloured sugar keeps well in these conditions.

Nuts are best chopped and toasted for use as a coating material. Chop with a long-bladed knife, and use the full width of the blade by grasping the tip of the knife in one hand and holding the handle firmly, use a see-saw action to chop. You can use a food processor for this job but the results tend to be more ground than chopped.

The chopped nuts should then be toasted lightly in the oven, under the grill or in a microwave. Remember, it is very easy to burn nuts, particularly when they are chopped, so watch them carefully, turning frequently to ensure even toasting. When cool, the chopped and toasted nuts can be used in the same way as vermicelli.

◆ Sugar ◆

Caster or granulated sugar can introduce a 'sparkling' appearance. Golden or 'harlequin' sugars are available in many supermarkets and can add colour to a white chocolate finish, and it is also possible to colour sugar at home with food colouring to exactly the shade you wish, as shown opposite.

◆ Coconut ◆

Coconut too can look very effective. Sweetened desiccated coconut stays fresh longer than the unsweetened type, so this is probably best to use for finishing chocolates. It looks very appetizing either left pure white or lightly toasted, but it can also be coloured in the same way as described for sugar, above.

◆ Chocolate ◆

It is easy to produce grated and flaked chocolate both of which give a nice textured finish. Chill a whole bar of chocolate in the refrigerator for at least an hour before attempting to grate it. Use a cheese grater and grate the chocolate on to a greaseproof sheet. The heat from your hand will make it impossible to grate the entire bar but the remainder can always be melted for dipping.

If you wish to flake the chocolate, chill the bar as above. Hold the chilled bar firmly in an upright position on a greaseproof sheet. With a sharp knife, cut slivers from the side of the bar using a downward action. You may have to re-chill the chocolate bar as this operation cannot be hurried and the chocolate may become soft as you work.

You can also always use a different-coloured chocolate to decorate a finished plain truffle. Try white strips on dark chocolate, or vice versa. Alternatively, one or two drops of food colouring in a little white chocolate will enable you to put a pink pattern on to a cherry brandy truffle, or orange on cointreau.

Dip your dipping fork into the contrasting chocolate and simply draw it across the top of the finished truffle, or use a piping bag fitted with a plain writing nozzle to produce a different pattern.

See pp. 86–92 for further ideas on chocolate finishes.

Finishing and Presentation

The effort that has gone into producing your own chocolates and sweets deserves care and attention in finishing, decoration, and presentation, whether you intend to serve what you have made to guests, to offer it as a gift, or sell it, perhaps at a fund-raising event. A little imagination will turn the simplest confections into joys for the eyes to behold. In this section you will find suggestions for ways to finish and decorate what you make, including advice on how to use chocolate itself as a luxury finishing touch for desserts and cakes, as well as confectionery. It is also possible to vary the way in which you present your chocolates to suit the occasion, and ideas are given here on how to use the ribbons, flowers and other seasonal decorations that will add the final stylish touch to any type of presentation.

• Decorating chocolates •

A simple way to decorate finished chocolates and sweets is to let them set completely after dipping, then mark them with a chocolate that contrasts – for instance plain chocolate on a finished milk chocolate and white on a plain or milk chocolate. It is also possible to colour white chocolate (see p. 13) to use in this way. The contrasting chocolate could be applied with the prongs of a dipping fork or ring, or drizzled over the finished chocolates. Alternatively, pipe contrasting chocolate decorations.

If you have a piping set, it is possible to pipe letters of the alphabet on to chocolate cups, or any moulded chocolate with a flat top. This can serve as an identification of the chocolate centre, 'B' for 'brandy', for example, 'R' for 'rum', 'C' for 'cherry', and so on; it can also serve to personalize the chocolates, particularly if they are a gift. A fun way to take this a stage further is to pack the chocolates in a flat box and pipe a name, or an endearment ('With Love', perhaps), or other greeting ('Happy Birthday' or 'Congratulations').

Tiny chocolate flowers (see p. 25), made in chocolate of any colour, make a pretty decoration for chocolates, as do sugar flowers, which are available from most supermarkets.

Small pieces of crystallized or glacé fruit (see pp. 57 and 59) can serve as an identification for chocolates, as well as a decoration. A piece of a crystallized orange or lemon slice, for instance, can be used to decorate an orange or lemon cream, while a piece of glacé cherry identifies a cherry fondant.

For rose and violet creams, in particular, candied rose petals, or violet flowers are the ideal finishing touch. With all these suggestions, always attach the finish immediately after dipping – chocolate quickly goes firm enough to stop any additions staying put.

Candied rose petals and whole violets and primulas make lovely finishing touches, for fondant fruit creams in particular. Cut pieces from the petals and flowers and attach straight after dipping.

◆ Candied flowers and petals ◆

If you are going to candy flowers and petals, you must pick flowers that are as close to perfect as possible, and candy them as soon after picking as possible. They must also be quite dry. Remember, too, that although many small flowers are suitable for candying, those that grow from bulbs are inedible. Once dry, candied flowers and petals will keep for some time in an airtight container. Cut pieces from them as decorations or use whole as garnishes.

Violets can be candied whole, but rose petals must be separated. Gently remove the petals and pinch out the yellow moon shape at the base of each petal. Gently paint both sides of the petals or flowers with lightly beaten egg white.

Lay each petal or flower in a dish of caster sugar and shake more sugar over the top. Lay the petals and flowers on a greaseproof-paper-lined tray and leave them in a warm place for at least 24 hours to dry. Turn several times during drying.

◆ Using chocolate ◆

Chocolate itself can be used as a finishing touch for other foods. Chocolate curls, for example, made as shown opposite, are particularly useful for decorating cakes and gateaux. It is, however, important to treat them with care and not to handle them unless you really must. Because they are so thin, the warmth of your hand is enough to melt them and cause them to lose their shape. Move them gently on a palette knife.

Chocolate shapes, cut with petits fours or biscuit cutters, made impressive finishing touches for cream-topped desserts, such as trifles, and an overlapping row of chocolate circles adds a look of luxury to a long cake or roulade. Chocolate squares form the basis of a tea-time treat. Bear in mind, when making any of these chocolate shapes, that breakages are almost inevitable. Simply melt the chocolate again and reuse it.

⋆ Chocolate decorations ⋆

Chocolate can be chopped, grated, flaked or curled to add texture and luxury to many confections. It is also possible to cut shapes from chocolate spread flat on to non-stick paper. For this you will need biscuit cutters, or an icing ruler and knife. A vegetable peeler and a cheese grater are also necessary. Chocolate to be grated or flaked should be well chilled; to be cut into shapes or curled, it should be at room temperature.

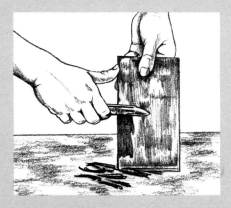

Chill a whole bar of chocolate before shaving off short curls with a vegetable peeler. Use a metal cheese grater for small flakes. Re-chill the chocolate as the heat from your hand makes it soft.

When working with chocolate spread on a flat surface, it should be at room temperature. The chocolate will curl away from the blade as you push a knife across the surface.

Petits fours and biscuit cutters produce an array of shapes; use an icing ruler and sharp knife for squares. This is best done when the chocolate is just firm.

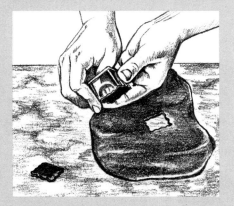

Slightly oil the cutters after each use to prevent them sticking next time. Ease the shapes gently from the cutters, but expect a percentage of breakages.

◆ Chocolate boxes ◆

Although time-consuming these little chocolate sponge cakes are a real treat! You will need a large number of chocolate squares – four for each chocolate box – made as described on p. 89.

MAKES 16 CHOCOLATE BOXES
one cooked sponge cake, about 20cm (8in) square
a little apricot jam
chocolate squares
115g (4oz) unsalted butter
170g (6oz) icing sugar
30g (1oz) cocoa powder
15ml (1tbsp) milk

1 Cool the sponge cake and cut it into 5cm (2in) squares. Spread a little sieved apricot jam on each side of the sponge squares, and press a chocolate square on to each side.

2 Make a rich chocolate butter cream. Beat the butter until soft. Sift together the icing sugar and cocoa powder and gradually beat it into the butter. Add enough milk to give a soft, piping consistency.

3 Fit a piping bag with a fluted nozzle and spoon the butter cream into it. Pipe a little butter cream on to the top of the little sponge cakes. If you wish, you could also add another chocolate square to give the boxes the appearance of a half-open lid.

◆ Seasonal finishing touches ◆

Seasonal finishes, particularly at Christmas, can be very eye-catching. Fudge Christmas puddings are favourites with both adults and children. For adults, make rum and raisin fudge (see p. 48) but before it is completely set, take about 115g (4oz) at a time and roll it into a round pudding. Allow it to set. Roll some fondant icing out thinly and cut little rounds to make 'white sauce' for the top of the pudding. Add a sprig of holly for the final touch. Children will probably prefer these puddings made with chocolate fudge (see p. 40).

Rum truffles are easily turned into miniature Christmas puddings with the addition of marzipan leaves and berries. Colour a little marzipan green and some red, cut out green leaf shapes, and roll mini red berries. Any white chocolate truffle can become a snowball if you dip it into more white chocolate, then roll it in sweetened desiccated coconut. A plateful of these puddings and snowballs makes a perfect end to the Christmas meal.

Marzipan 'chocolate' holly leaves make a seasonal finishing touch to a selection of Christmas chocolates. Knead a little cocoa powder into the marzipan, and cut out large leaves with a cutter if you have one, or the tip of a teaspoon. Attach silver berries (available from supermarkets).

Christmas treats. The large pudding in the foreground is rum and raisin fudge,
the smaller ones traditional rum truffles, all topped with fondant icing and marzipan leaves and berries.

• Chocolate leaves •

These make a lovely finishing touch to a plate of dipped fruits and are easy to make without using moulds or any special equipment. All you need is a selection of fresh leaves and some melted chocolate. Rose leaves are really the best to use, but you can use geranium or bay leaves, or the leaf from any non-poisonous plant. You can make mint leaves simply by adding a drop or two of peppermint oil to the chocolate before painting the leaves.

Try to choose leaves with clearly defined veins as these will look very impressive. Wash and dry them thoroughly. With an artist's brush, paint the melted chocolate on to the underside of the leaf, taking care to go to the very edge, but not over it. Place the leaves on a tray in a cool place to dry completely. Allow about three to four hours in a cool place.

When the chocolate is completely dry, carefully remove the leaf. If you find that the chocolate is too thin and begins to break or crack, paint another thin coat of melted chocolate over the first, and again allow to dry. It is not advisable to put the leaves in the refrigerator, as the very cold air makes them brittle and they will not readily peel from the chocolate.

• Serving chocolates •

Your chocolates will always be at their best if they are eaten as soon as possible after making. For a dinner party, chocolates are best served on a pretty plate or dish that is easy to pass around. An open dish on your table is also tempting, and guests will more readily help themselves from it than they would from a box. An unusual touch for a larger party is to buy some small boxes that will hold two chocolates each, put two contrasting chocolates inside and tie the boxes prettily. Write the guests' names on the boxes before placing them around the table. This will be a novel place-finder, and your guests can either eat the chocolates as petits fours or take them home.

◆ Chocolates as gifts ◆

To present a personal gift of chocolates, a pretty box decorated with ribbons will always be greeted with delight. There are many types of box available in the shops – plain and fancy – which will serve the purpose very well. A plain box with a colourful ribbon bow is a good combination, and gold or silver packages will give the recipient a hint of the luxury to be found inside. Also available in many gift shops are good-to-keep decorated tins. These are perfect for sweets like toffees or fudge which need to be kept in airtight conditions to prevent stickiness. Layer the sweets between pieces of waxed paper or, better still, wrap each piece individually, first in waxed paper or parchment, then twist coloured cellophane around before packing. Once wrapped in this way, fudge and toffees keep well and need not necessarily be packed in a tin.

A little china or glass plate or dish – a gift in itself – becomes even more special when filled with home-made confectionery. Place a lacy doily on the plate before filling it with chocolates. Try wrapping one or two chocolates in gold foil to add a touch of luxury. Cover both plate and chocolates tightly with cling film and, finally, add a frothy bow to complete a perfect gift.

◆ Stylish presentation ◆

The presentation of a box of chocolates for a gift is almost as important as the chocolates themselves! It is possible to buy many types of boxes in an array of colours and sizes suitable for sweets.

Do not cram in too many chocolates, but fill the box so that the contents cannot roll about inside. Tie coloured ribbons both ways round the box and secure firmly by tying them together.

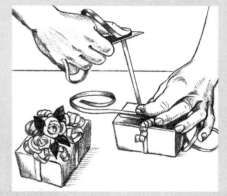

Curl thin ribbon by stretching it away from the box and running the blade of a knife or scissors along its length. Gently ease the curled ribbons into a frothy-looking bow.

An edible box, made of chocolate and with a mould, is another luxurious way to present chocolates (see pp. 14–19). Either make just the lid and use that as a little dish or make a whole chocolate box, fill it with chocolates, wrap it loosely in tissue paper, and place in a gift box.

Half of an Easter egg filled with home-made sweets makes a special Easter gift. Partly fill the inside of the egg with dark tissue paper to make a soft bed for the filling; if you don't, the chocolates at the very bottom may be crushed. Tightly wrap the egg with cling film to protect it from atmospheric changes.

At Christmas time, of course, crackers are a useful and seasonal way to present home-made chocolates. It is possible to buy crackers specially to fill with your own gifts. Four or five luxury chocolates in a little cellophane bag, tied with ribbons, make a perfect stocking filler acceptable to either sex.

Another festive presentation is to pack chocolates into a box and decorate it with tinsel and holly. Marzipan fruits, and crystallized and glacé fruits, all make lovely seasonal treats.

◆ Packaging goods to sell ◆

If you have made chocolates or sweets to sell at a fête or fair, there are one or two additional points you should remember when packing them.

Firstly, it is best to use inexpensive packaging materials. A foil freezer-type container with a doily placed in the bottom, filled with sweets, then wrapped tightly in cling film, makes a good package. Alternatively, cut a large circle of bright tissue paper. In the centre of the circle, place a number of sweets, individually wrapped in waxed paper. Gather the tissue around the sweets and tie with ribbon, just above the sweets, to make a handkerchief-like parcel. A package like this made with clear, coloured cellophane is equally effective.

Second, *always* wrap or cover completely any foodstuff that you are offering for sale – no-one will want to buy sweets that have been handled or breathed over. The third point to take into consideration is labelling. If the contents of a package are not visible, clearly mark on the outside what is in the pack. Be accurate when weighing, and put the weight somewhere on the pack, stating whether it is net weight (the goods only) or gross (the whole pack).

However you decide to present your own chocolates, always treat them with care and respect. Keep all sweets cool, and out of direct sunlight. Remember to serve contrasting colours and different textures together to bring added interest to your confectionery – chocolate-covered brazil nuts with a soft-centred chocolate or some chocolate cherries, perhaps.

The prettier the package or the more attractive the presentation, the more pleasure your home-made confectionery will give.

Presentation is all important, particularly if you are offering your home-made confectionery as a gift. Boxes and gift bags are available in all shapes and sizes, and ribbons complete the effect. Gold and silver gift wrap and boxes offer a hint of the luxury to be found inside.

Index